ABT

DISCARDED

5.00

P9-AFY-373

Fodor's CITYPACK

NAPLES'
25 BEST

WITH FULL-SIZE
FOLDOUT MAP

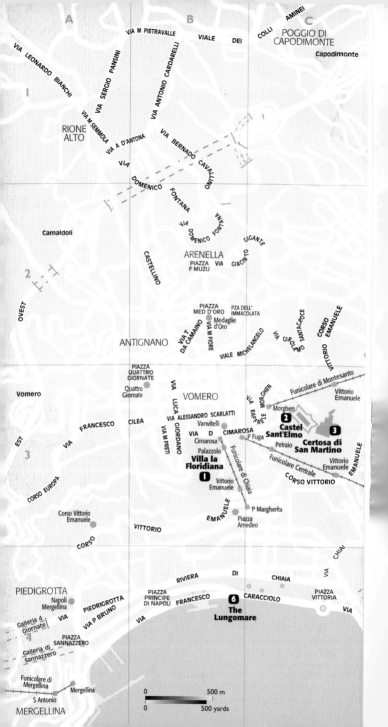

Top 25 locator map
(continues on inside
back cover)

←

Fodor's CITYPACK
NAPLES' 25 BEST

by Michael Buttler

Fodor's Travel Publications
New York • Toronto •
London • Sydney • Auckland
www.fodors.com

About This Book

KEY TO SYMBOLS

✛ Map reference to the Top 25 locator map

✉ Address

☎ Telephone number

🕓 Opening/closing times

🍴 Restaurant or café on premises or nearby

🚉 Nearest railway station

Ⓜ Nearest Metro (subway) station

🚌 Nearest bus route

🚢 Nearest riverboat or ferry stop

♿ Facilities for visitors with disabilities

✋ Admission charges: Expensive (over €6), Moderate (€2–6) and Inexpensive (€2 or less).

↔ Other nearby places of interest

❓ Other practical information

➤ Indicates the page where you will find a fuller description

ℹ Tourist information

ORGANIZATION

This guide is divided into six sections:

- Planning Ahead, Getting There
- Living Naples—Naples Now, Naples Then, Time to Shop, Out and About, Walks, Naples by Night
- Naples' Top 25 Sights
- Naples' Best—best of the rest
- Where To—detailed listings of restaurants, hotels, shops and nightlife
- Travel Facts—practical information

In addition, easy-to-read side panels provide extra facts and snippets, highlights of places to visit and invaluable practical advice.

The colours of the tabs on the page corners match the colours of the triangles aligned with the chapter names on the contents page opposite.

MAPS

The Top 25 locator map found on the inside front and back covers of the book itself is for quick reference. It shows the Top 25 Sights, described on pages 26–50, which are clearly plotted by number (**1**–**25**, not page number) in the author's suggested viewing order. The grid reference given for the Top 25 Sights refers to this map. **The fold-out map** in the wallet at the back of this book is a comprehensive street plan of Naples.

Contents

Planning Ahead

WHEN TO GO

The best time to visit Naples is between May and September. The very best month is May, because of Maggio dei Monumenti (see below). August is best avoided, partly because of the heat, but also because many shops, restaurants, clubs and bars close for all or part of the month. December is the time when people descend to buy *presepi* (Christmas crèches). The atmosphere is wonderful, but there is no room to move.

TIME

Naples is one hour ahead of GMT, six hours ahead of New York and nine hours ahead of Los Angeles. Clocks go forward one hour for summer time.

AVERAGE DAILY MAXIMUM TEMPERATURES

JAN	FEB	MAR	APR	MAY	JUN	JUL	AUG	SEP	OCT	NOV	DEC
53°F	53°F	59°F	65°F	72°F	79°F	84°F	86°F	81°F	70°F	61°F	55°F
12°C	12°C	15°C	18°C	22°C	26°C	29°C	30°C	27°C	21°C	16°C	13°C

Spring (March–May) is generally mild and pleasant, with occasional short showers in March and April.
Summer (June–August) can be baking hot, especially in August when it is best to go to the coast.
Autumn (September–October) is very pleasant, with warm days and occasional cloud.
Winter (November–February) can be sunny and crisp with some dull weather and rain.

WHAT'S ON

January *Epiphany* (5/6 Jan): The *Befana* witch gives candies to the children in Piazza del Plebiscito, and celebrations continue over the city.
April *Holy Week*: Involves Good Friday processions with the various brotherhoods, church concerts and a day off on Easter Monday.
May *Maggio dei Monumenti*: Churches, palaces, artists' workshops and public buildings are open to the public free of charge.
San Gennaro (first Sun in month): The liquefaction of the saint's blood takes place

at a service in the Duomo, followed by a street procession from the Duomo and back.
July *Festival of Madonna del Carmine* (16 Jul): Celebrated with a firework display near the church campanile.
Neapolis Festival (last week): One of the best rock and pop music festivals in Italy.
August *Ferragosto* (Feast of the Assumption, 15 Aug): Marked with celebrations all over the city.
September *Pizzafest* (first two weeks): More pizzas than ever are produced and

eaten during the event's two weeks that end on 19 Sep.
San Gennaro (19 Sep): The main celebration of the liquefaction of the saint's blood takes place in the Duomo, followed by a procession to Piazza del Carmine.
December *Christmas:* Crowds come to buy *presepi* (Christmas crèches) in Via Gregorio Armeno, and many examples can be seen in the churches.
Capodanno (New Year's Eve): Concert and fireworks in Piazza del Plebiscito.

NAPLES ONLINE
www.agendaonline.it/napoli/naples.htm
An interesting site with a great deal of information about leisure, bars and clubs, as well as visitor attractions.

www.anm.it
This site has bus information, and has the complete details of each line's destination.

www.beniculturali.it
The National Ministry of Culture has a comprehensive site (with some parts translated into English), and carries plenty of information about all the visitor attractions in the area.

www.campaniartecard.it
The *Campania Artecard*, that indispensable discount card for visiting the major attractions in the city and Campi Flegrei, has a useful site with full details of how to obtain the card.

www.enit.it
The Italian Tourist Board has a good range of useful information about the whole of Italy including Naples.

www.inaples.it
The Naples Tourist Board site has good information about all aspects of visiting the city, from museums to shopping and sport, and is in six languages.

www.metro.na.it
Metronapolis runs the Metro (subway) and the funiculars, and this useful site gives routes and fares, as well as information about the modern art appearing in some Metro stations.

www.napolinapoli.com
A comprehensive guide to what's on and places to go. It is mostly in Italian, although there are some comic English translations.

www.10best.com
An independent site with some useful recommendations about what to see and where to go.

GOOD TRAVEL SITES

www.fodors.com
A travel-planning site where you can research where to go, prices and local weather as well as book flights, hotels and car rental. There is also feedback from other users together with links to other sites.

www.tripadvisor.com
A useful site with information about what to see and how to travel, as well as hotel bookings. Has a good section on Naples.

www.trenitalia.it
Indispensable site for anyone planning to travel by train in Italy.

www.virtualtourist.com
Interesting for its frank comments from visitors about what they did or did not enjoy in the city.

CYBERCAFÉS

Cybercafés come and go regularly, so check before you visit.
Internet Bar ✚ Piazza Bellini ☎ 081 295 237
Multimedia ✚ Via San Giovanni Maggiore a Pignatelli 34 ☎ 081 551 4708; Internetcafenapoli @yahoo.it
Dre@mer Club ✚ Vico San Domenico Maggiore 7 ☎ No phone
ClicNet ✚ Via Toledo 393 ☎ 081 552 9370

Getting There

ENTRY REQUIREMENTS

All visitors to Italy require a valid passport. Visas are not required for UK, US, Australian, Canadian, Irish, New Zealand or other EU nationals, provided the stay is no longer than three months, but always check prior to a visit and follow news events that may affect your situation. EU nationals receive free or reduced cost medical treatment with the qualifying document (for UK citizens, the E111/EHIC). Otherwise private medical insurance cover is wise.

MONEY

The Italian currency is the euro, with notes of €5, €10, €20, €50, €100, €200 and €500 and coins of €2 (gold with silver surround), €1 (silver with gold surround); 1 cent, 2 cents, 5 cents (bronze coloured); 10 cents, 20 cents and 50 cents (all gold coloured).

€50

€100

ARRIVING

A number of airlines from Europe, including the UK, fly direct to Naples' Capodichino airport. Intercontinental flights generally go to Rome or Milan, so a connecting flight (or even a train) will be required.

FROM CAPODICHINO AIRPORT

The airport is relatively small and only 7km (4 miles) from central Naples. For flight information ☎ 848 888 777; www.gesac.it. There are several shops, ATMs and bars. The best way to get from the airport into the city is to use an *Alibus*. They depart every 30 minutes and the journey to Piazza Garibaldi takes 15 minutes. The buses also go to the port terminal at Piazza Municipio. The fare is €3. The return journey starts from Corso Novara. A taxi should cost no more than €20, but be sure to take one of the official taxis with the city badge on the front door.

ARRIVING BY CAR

For visitors wishing to drive overland through Europe, Naples is about 1,750km (1,050 miles) from London, and the A1 from Rome is a good, fast approach. Dual carriageways (divided highways) bypass the city on the way to the coastal resorts, or the Amalfi Coast.

ARRIVING BY BUS

Long-distance buses from London go to Rome, where it is necessary to change bus for Naples.

This is a long journey, but eventually you will arrive in Piazza Garibaldi. There is an information desk in the piazza.

ARRIVING BY TRAIN
Trains from all over Italy arrive at Napoli Centrale station in Piazza Garibaldi, which is the interchange for most other local services. To travel on to Sorrento or Pompei, however, it is necessary to change to the Circumvesuviana station.

GETTING AROUND
Buses: The easiest way to get around the city and out to Mergellina and Posillipo. GiraNapoli tickets can be bought from *tabacchi*. There are two types of tickets: One valid for 90 minutes and the other for one day, and they can also be used on the Metro (www.anm.it).

Funicolare (funicular): Good for getting up Vomero hill. Centrale line goes from Augusteo (on Via Toledo) to Piazza Fuga via Corso Vittorio Emanuele and Petraio. Montesanto line goes from Piazza Montesanto to Via Morghen. Mergellina line goes from Via Mergellina to Via Alessandro Manzoni. Tickets are bought at the stations.

Metro: Especially convenient for more distant areas. There are two lines and considerable work is under way to create more stations. Some stations (Dante, Museo, Materdei and Salvator Rosa) are showcases for modern art. GiraNapoli tickets (€3) from *tabacchi* can also be used on buses.

Taxis: Registered taxis are white with the city badge on the front door. There is a minimum charge per trip, with extra charges for luggage, journeys after 10pm or on a Sunday, and to the airport. The cost on a long journey will include the return trip. Tip 15–20 per cent.

Trains: Local train *Ferrovia Cumana* runs from Piazza Montesanto to Campi Flegrei (Torregaveta). *Ferrovia Circumvesuviana* runs from Corso Giuseppe Garibaldi to Ercolano (Herculaneum), Pompei and Sorrento.

INSURANCE
Check your policy and buy any necessary supplements. It is vital that travel insurance covers medical expenses, in addition to accident, trip cancellation, baggage loss and theft. Check the policy covers any continuing treatment for a chronic condition.

VISITORS WITH DISABILITIES
It is not easy for visitors with restricted mobility to make the most of Naples. Many streets are uneven and there are few ramps. Streets with steps are common in this hilly city, and most of the churches and other attractions have steps. A few concessions are made, but they are sporadic and not very well thought out.

DRIVING IN NAPLES
Driving in central Naples is only for the intrepid. Narrow streets, uneven surfaces and the brio of the Italian drivers all make for a most unnerving experience. It is better to park and use public transport.

Living
Naples

Naples Now

Above: *Fish is a popular and regular choice of food for Neapolitans, and the evocative Mercato Porta Nolana is one of the best places in the city to find it*

The romantic view of Naples is that it is exuberant, full of characters who shout and sing Neapolitan love songs at every turn, dirty and crowded, with too much crime, but set in a priceless location with superb food and an uninhibited love of life. Much of that is true, but Naples is more than a romantic stereotype.

Since 1993, the city has pulled itself up by its bootstraps. The mayor, Antonio Bassolino, invested huge sums in a civic makeover, which smartened up several areas, improved the city's self-esteem, and raised its profile abroad. Visitors are coming in increasing numbers to appreciate what a special city Naples is.

Part of its appeal lies in the fact that it is a living, breathing city, not a museum piece or a work of art. There are certainly some obvious fine monuments here, but there are also treasures hidden away in dusty old churches that take a bit of seeking out. Where else would Caravaggio's masterpiece *Seven Acts of Mercy* be tucked away in a tiny church that is not open half the time! The Neapolitans take their rich artistic heritage in their stride and, step by step, are bringing it to

Above: *The sumptuous
interior of the Duomo, site
of San Gennaro miracles*
Left: *The Scalone d'Onore,
in the majestic and important
Palazzo Reale*

our attention. An excellent scheme is the *Maggio
dei Monumenti* in May when dozens of buildings, normally closed, are opened up, concerts
are held in some of the most beautiful rooms
and churches in the city, and other cultural
events are going on all around the city. Another
good initiative is the *Campania Artecard*, which
offers a range of discount cards providing either
free or reduced price admission to 11 attractions
in Naples itself plus 35 other sites, including
Pompei and Ercolana (Herculaneum), outside
the city. It also allows discounts on concert
tickets and free transport throughout the area. In
these and in many other ways the city is opening
up its heritage for the world to see.

VITTORIO DE SICA

● Born in 1901 and
raised in Naples, De
Sica began his career
on the stage. He starred
in his first film in 1932,
and became a director
in 1939. After World
War II, he directed
The Gold of Naples
starring Sophia Loren.
Several of his gritty,
realistic films won
Academy awards.

11

Above: *Sanctuary at Piazza San Domenico Maggiore—a peaceful shrine in the hustle and bustle of Naples*

PULCINELLA

• The masked clown, who is in turn carefree and miserable, was a famous part of the *Commedia del Arte*, the style of popular theatrical performance developed in Naples. He has come to represent the archetypal Neapolitan, and Pulcinella dolls have become popular souvenirs.

Naples appeals to more senses than merely the eyes, however. It has a strong appeal to the ears as well. Apart from the racket in the streets—car horns, motorcycles, radios, traders yelling—there is always music in the air. Buskers on street corners, groups rehearsing in upstairs rooms, organists playing in the churches, they all reflect the people's enjoyment of music. Of course, there is a long tradition of Neapolitan song, with such classics as *O' Sole Mio* and *Funiculi Funiculà*, a tradition kept alive in the Teatro Trianon (► 84), and in the Neapolitan song contest in Piedigrotta in September. Opera has always been the city's great love, and the Teatro San Carlo (► 35) is second only to Milan's La Scala in Italy. From Rossini and Donizetti, the foremost musicians in the world have played in Naples, and the audiences have shown their approval when they felt it was deserved. They did not give it to poor Caruso who, after being hissed here, never sang in Naples again.

For many, Naples' greatest attraction is its food. The city that gave us pizzas, spaghetti and ice cream continues to spoil us today. It is easy to gain the impression, as you walk around, that

Neapolitans spend all their time eating! From first thing in the morning, with their hasty espresso and *cornetto* (croissant) eaten on the move, to mid-morning, when there are plenty of cakes to tempt them, and lunchtime, when they might grab a slice of pizza or some *friggitore* (fried snacks, such as *zucchini*). Those with more time to spare might indulge in something from the *tavola calda*, a buffet of hot food that can include some real delicacies. Mid-afternoon is time for another pastry, perhaps one of the city's traditional *sfogliatelle* or a rum baba. There is always room, however, for a healthy dinner mid-evening. Fish is a regular choice, particularly since we are by the sea. Pizzas here are somehow lighter and crisper than any

Above: *Piazza San Domenico Maggiore—relaxing with friends and refreshments is one of the Neapolitans' most popular pastimes*

SOPHIA LOREN

- Although she was actually born in Rome in 1934, Sophia Loren very soon moved with her mother to Pozzuoli. Brought up in poverty, she started winning beauty contests in her teens and was spotted by Carlo Ponti. At the age of 18 she starred as a pizza girl in *The Gold of Naples*, and never looked back.

13

Above: *Young Neapolitans respect festival traditions*

ENRICO CARUSO

• One of Naples' most famous sons, Caruso did not, in fact, spend much of his life in the city. Born in 1873, he became the finest boy contralto in Naples, but at the age of 28 he was hissed off the stage at Teatro San Carlo (➤ 35), and vowed never to return to sing in Naples. However, at the age of 48, suffering from pleurisy, he died while staying overnight at the Hotel Vesuvio. He was then celebrated in the city as a long-lost son.

others, and there are endless types of pasta, with delicious sauces. Neapolitan cooking mostly reflects the rustic traditions of the Campania region, with plenty of tomatoes, beans, mozzarella cheese, garlic and fresh herbs. It will be hard to find a poor meal in Naples, given the passion, lifelong interest and sheer love of food that almost everybody possesses.

For all their unselfconscious camaraderie, Neapolitans have a strong sense of style. The most famous names in the fashion world have shops here, but even the department stores sell extremely chic lines. Any social gathering will be full of people looking like advertising models, and many of them look like this all the time! During the evenings and at the weekends, people are out enjoying themselves and looking fantastic. The bars and nightclubs fill up towards midnight, when everyone wants to see and be seen. A number of the more fashionable clubs are out of the city, in Posillipo, Pozzuoli or even further, and the roads get jammed with people looking for a good time. *Neapolis*, one of the best pop and rock festivals in Italy, takes place in July every year in the Bagnoli area.

There is no denying that Neapolitans live life to the full, in spite of the terrible travails the city has been through over the years. Some say that living in the shadow of Vesuvio (Vesuvius—which may still erupt at any time and overwhelm those foolish enough to be living on its slopes) breeds a certain fatalism, which encourages everyone to live for the moment. Few cities in Europe have suffered such misery, even since World War II. Devastated by bombing, half-hearted attempts at regenerating the city bred widespread criminality and black-market racketeering. There were severe outbreaks of cholera in 1944 and as recently as 1973, and corrupt city governments did nothing to stop the ugly building developments that can be seen all over the city. There are still pockets of terrible poverty in the Quartieri Spagnoli. And the *Camorra*, Naples' version of the Mafia, still controls over half the business in the city. This is the side that the visitor does not see, but it may help us to understand the character of the people. We see their charm, their sense of fun, their love of food and of singing, their kindness towards children and their pride in the city's history. They bring the city to life.

Above: *The imposing roof of the stylish Galleria Umberto I*

DIEGO MARADONA

- An honorary Neapolitan, Maradona came from Argentina in 1984 to join Napoli SSC soccer team and pulled them up to record heights. Within three years they had won the championship of Serie A, the Italian top division. In 1989 they won the UEFA Cup, followed by the Serie A championship again in 1990. Never had they seen such success, and Maradona is still admired by the people.

15

Naples Then

From left to right: *The Bay of Naples from Mateaux's Peeps Abroad for Folks At Home (1872);*
The homeless beggars of Naples from Peeps Abroad for Folks At Home (1872);
Lady Hamilton painted by Tischbein

REVOLUTION IN NAPLES

The 1789 French Revolution also sparked ideas of republicanism in Naples, which was under French rule at the time, and the king and queen of Naples panicked and fled to Sicily. A group of well-educated idealists persuaded the French army that a republic was the best way to avoid anarchy. The Parthenopean Republic was declared on 23 January 1799, but it was short lived, and after some fierce battles with the king's forces, an armistice was declared. Despite assurances of free passage, most of the leaders were tried and executed.

c800BC	Greeks found Cumae, then Parthenope (680BC) on Pizzofalcone.
c470BC	Greek settlers found Neapolis.
326BC	Romans conquer Naples.
89–82BC	Neapolitans rebel against Rome, but are brutally crushed.
AD79	Vesuvio erupts and buries Pompei (►50) and Ercolano (►20).
455	Goths and Vandals conquer Campania and Naples.
536	Byzantine Emperor Justinian occupies Naples.
1062	Normans launch attack from Capua to control southern Italy.
1139	Naples swears allegiance to Norman Sicily, which now controls much of Southern Italy.
1266	Charles d'Anjou installs French regime, and builds Castel Nuovo (►41).
1442	King of Aragon drives out Angevins to begin 365 years of Spanish rule.
1600	Naples, Europe's largest city, has a population of over 300,000.

1631 The city is devastated by another Vesuvio eruption.

1656 Plague kills 75 per cent of the population.

1734 The French enter the city and give Charles III the Kingdom of Sicily (including Naples).

1735–59 Bourbon King Charles III develops Naples, building Capodimonte Palace (► 37) and Teatro San Carlo (► 35), and excavates Pompei and Ercolano.

1793 Horatio Nelson arrives in Naples and meets Emma Hamilton.

1860 Garibaldi enters Naples, and the city votes for a unified Italian kingdom, ruled by Victor Emanuele II of Savoy.

1884 Naples is devastated by cholera.

1922 Fascists replace 'popular block' city government with Catholic conservatives.

1943 Allied bombs leave Centro Storico in ruins before invasion via Salerno.

1944 Vesuvio erupts, killing 26. Naples votes to retain monarchy, but also provides first president, Enrico de Nicola, for new Italian republic (1946).

1973 Naples is again hit by cholera.

1980 Earthquake in Campania kills 3,000.

1994 Renovation of historical monuments under mayor. G7 summit held here.

2004 Improvements in the city continue, with expansion of the Metro system, and updating of the port.

NELSON AND LADY HAMILTON

The hero of the British Navy, Captain Horatio Nelson, entered Naples' waters in 1793 in search of additional supplies. Britain's ambassador, Sir William Hamilton, greeted him and introduced him to his wife, Emma. Little did he know what a scandalous series of events he had set in motion. Following his victory at the Battle of the Nile in 1798, Nelson returned to Naples and stayed with the Hamiltons. Before long, there was talk of an affair between Nelson and Emma Hamilton. He stayed on in Naples, against the orders of the British Admiralty, and enjoyed a lavish social life. Everywhere the couple went in Europe, they were greeted with tremendous affection. Eventually Nelson was sent to the Baltic while Emma was pregnant with his daughter, and in 1805 he died at the Battle of Trafalgar.

17

Time to Shop

Naples can offer everything from cut-price markets to designer window-shopping

Whatever you want to buy you should be able to find it in Naples. The shops range from the stylish to the disorganized, from aloof to entertaining, and from hyper-expensive to

bargain priced. Energetic and chaotic, the shopping experience is enhanced by the markets (► 57), found in different parts of the city.

OPENING TIMES

Most shops open between 8.30am and 9am Monday to Friday, sometimes later on Saturday (10am). Almost all close at around 1.30 until 4.30 and then stay open until 7pm or 8pm. Many close on Monday mornings and Saturday afternoons. Food shops often close on Thursday afternoons and Saturday afternoons. A few open on Sunday mornings. In August, however, many shops and other businesses close for all or part of the month.

The height of fashion can be found in the area around Piazza dei Martiri (► 74) and along Via Alabardieri, where there are some big names like Armani, Prada and Ferragamo. Via Chiaia, which also leads out of the Piazza dei Martiri, is full of smart shops, and smart people. Via Toledo is a popular, pedestrianized street, with slightly cheaper clothes, but for the bargains, head for Corso Umberto I (► 58). A less hectic area is Vomero, where there is the stylish Galleria Scarlatti in Via Alessandro Scarlatti. A number of boutiques have outlets here, and there is also the Coin department store in the same street. For really cheap clothes, head north from here to the Mercatino di Antignano (► 57) in Piazza degli Artisti.

Smart items for the home are available in many places, but the area that is most rewarding is

Chiaia. In the narrow streets around Vico Belledonne a Chiaia there are dozens of little shops with unusual glass, ceramics, lamps and furnishings and other unique pieces, some

From eclectic antiques to the ultra-modern boutiques on Via Chiaia, Naples has it all

CHOICE SOUVENIRS

Special presents that are unique to the city or the area are the following.
Cheese: Campania is the home of mozzarella, but also look for scamorza.
Chocolate: The gorgeous creations in Gay Odin (► 75) are irresistible.
Coral: It may be expensive, but coral jewellery from this area is particularly fine.
Limoncello: Delicious lemon-tasting liqueur, available from a shop where it is made (► 75).
Pulcinella doll: The masked clown that represents the Neapolitan character (► 12).
Shoes: Stylish shoes are everywhere in the city, but unusual ones can be found (for a price) at Aldo Tramontano (► 74), who is based here.
Wine: Among the many good local wines, particularly special is Lacryma Christi, grown on the slopes of Vesuvio.

modern and some antique. For really valuable antiques, head for Vico Santa Maria Vecchia, off Piazza dei Martiri.

Souvenirs that more reflect the soul of the city can be found in Centro Storico, along Via dei Tribunali and Spaccanapoli (► 43). The famous *presepi* (Christmas crèches) are sold by almost every shop in Via San Gregorio Armeno, along with Pulcinella dolls and masks. Delicatessen foods (such as cold meats and breads) either to eat or take home can also be found here, but the freshest food and the best variety will be found at one of the markets (► 57), where you can join the high-octane market shopper.

Out and About

Below: *Ercolano's Casa di Nettuno e Anfitrite*
Below right: *Looking down on Sorrento's rocky coastline*

UNDERGROUND NAPLES

One of the most fascinating aspects of the city's history is its network of underground tunnels and aqueducts. Conducted tours of these chambers are led by Napolisotteranea (✉ Piazza San Gaetano 68 ☎ 081 296 944; www.napolisotterranea.org). The tours last about one and a half hours. Another tour of Acquedotto Carmignano starts from Caffè Gambrinus (➤ 68), and visits the tunnels used as air-raid shelters (☎ 081 400 256; www.lanapolisotterranea.it).

INFORMATION

VESUVIO (VESUVIUS)
Distance 16km (10 miles)
Travel time 30 minutes
www.parks.it
☎ 081 777 5720
🕐 Daily 9–5
🚆 Ferrovia Circumvesuviana from station in Corso Garibaldi to Torre Annunziata
🎫 Moderate
❓ By car, take the A3 Naples to Salerno road and exit at Ercolano or Torre del Greco, then follow Vesuvio signs.

ORGANIZED SIGHTSEEING
Guided bus tours to see Naples by night are organized every Friday evening from November to April by the Chamber of Commerce, with tickets available from travel agencies and hotel desks. They also arrange tours to Campi Flegrei on alternate Saturdays during the same period.

Boat trips around the bay depart from Molo Bevellero.

VESUVIO (VESUVIUS)
The walk up the 1,281-m (4,203-foot) volcano starts from the parking area and takes about 30 minutes. It is worth visiting the Museo dell'Osservatorio Vesuviano to understand the volcano's geology and when it may erupt again. The edge of the crater provides a very dramatic view inside, and there are also a few other footpaths through the national park.

ERCOLANO (HERCULANEUM)
Much smaller than Pompei, but better preserved thanks to the sea of mud that engulfed it in AD79, Ercolano is still only partly excavated. What does exist is fascinating. This was a residential town, and several of the houses show signs of considerable wealth. The Casa dei Cervi has a well-preserved upper storey as well as a garden courtyard. The mosaic floor at the Casa dell'Atrio a Mosaico is spectacular, and there are some charming mosaics in Casa di Nettuno e Anfitrite.

SORRENTO

This peaceful, pretty, seaside resort seems a million miles from the bustle of Naples, yet it does not take long to reach it. The maze of narrow streets to the west of Piazza Tasso with their shops selling the typical *intarsio* work (inlaid marquetry) is fascinating to explore. Visit

the Sedile Dominova (now a working men's club) to see the 15th-century frescoes. There's a steep walk down to the sea, but Marina Grande makes a pleasant place to laze. Just as steep is the walk up out of the town to the rocky hills, but there are plenty of clearly marked pathways providing impressive views across the peninsula.

CAPRI

This beautiful island is at least as famous as its many glittering visitors, and is well worth a visit. The big draw is the Grotta Azzurra (Blue Grotto), accessible from the Marina Grande. At the opposite end of the island, Villa Jovis is where Emperor Tiberius moved the seat of government, while the terraced gardens of the Giardini di Augusto are an oasis of vibrant flowers. Capri town itself is reached by funicular from the Marina Grande and buzzes with celebrity life, especially around the Piazzetta. Less grand is Anacapri, set high overlooking the whole island. Originally a rural settlement, it is now getting very busy, but you can still escape the crowds by walking up to the nature reserve on the hill.

INFORMATION

ERCOLANO (HERCULANEUM)
Distance 12km (8 miles)
Travel time 30 minutes
081 739 0963
Daily 9am–2 hours before dusk
Ferrovia Circumvesuviana from station in Corso Garibaldi to Ercolana-Scavi
Moderate
By car, take the A3 Naples to Salerno road and exit at Ercolano.

INFORMATION

SORRENTO
Distance 48km (29 miles)
www.sorrentotourism.it
081 807 4033
Ferrovia Circumvesuviana from station in Corso Garibaldi to Sorrento
Hydrofoil or ferry from Molo Beverello and from Mergellina
By car, take the A3 Naples to Salerno road, exit at Castellammare di Stabia and then follow Statale 145 to Sorrento.

INFORMATION

CAPRI
Distance 25km (15 miles)
www.caprionline.com
081 837 0686
Hydrofoil or ferry from Molo Beverello and from Mergellina.

Walks

INFORMATION

Distance 3km (2 miles)
Time 1.5 hours
Start point Castel
dell'Ovo
🚍 140, C9, C10, C24,
C25, C28, R3
End point Chiesa di Santa
Maria del Parto,
Mergellina
🚍 C16, C24, R3

WALK 1 ALONG THE LUNGOMARE

Walk along Via Partenope with the sea on your left, past the Grand Hotel Vesuvius and after two bends in the road you will reach Piazza Vittoria, where all the buses stop. Cross the road at the traffic lights to enter the Villa Comunale, the pleasant 18th-century royal gardens. Walk along the cobbles, and notice the splendid umbrella pine trees, typical of the Campania region. To the left is the waterfront, and to the right is Riviera di Chiaia. After about 200m (218 yards), you reach the first of several fountains, this one surrounded by four lions. Further along, on the left, is the Stazione Zoologica (Acquario), just in front of which there is an ornate bandstand in green pewter and iron, with hanging glass globes.

At this point, turn left towards the sea and leave the park near one of the small cafés. Turn right along Via Francesco Caracciolo, and then very soon Via Anton Dohrn will bear off to the right, but the walk keeps left along the waterfront. This is the most convenient place to stop and visit Museo Villa Pignatelli. Otherwise continue along Via Francesco Caracciolo, passing, on the right, a statue with a soldier on horseback. In about 300m (327 yards) pass the Piazza della Repubblica and continue along the waterfront towards the Porticciolo di Mergellina. After an ice cream from one of the chalets, walk up (or take the lift/elevator from 9B Via Francesco Caracciolo) to visit the little church of Santa Maria del Parto (► 55), with its wonderful view across the bay.

There are plenty of pretty views of the bay to be enjoyed

WALK 2 FROM THE COAST TO THE HISTORIC CITY

From Piazza del Plebiscito, walk north into the adjoining Piazza Trieste e Trento with its busy cafés and leave from the top right corner of the piazza along Via San Carlo past the elegant Galleria Umberto I on the left and Teatro San Carlo on the right. Take the first road on the left, Via Giuseppe Verdi, which leads to Piazza Municipio, where there is a statue of King Emanuele II, unified Italy's first king. The City Hall is situated on the west side of the piazza, and to the right of this building is the Chiesa di San Giacomo degli Spagnoli. Just to the right of the church is a narrow street, Via San Giacomo, which leads to Via Toledo. Turn right along this broad, semi-pedestrianized street with its smart clothes shops and tempting patisseries.

The poor area of Quartieri Spagnoli is to the left. Notice some of the grand *palazzi* on either side of the street and continue as far as Piazza Carità. One side of the piazza is dominated by the huge Post Office, built in the 1930s. There is a striking war memorial facing it. Take the road in the top right corner, Via Mario Morgantini, which leads into Piazza Monteoliveto, with the police station and Chiesa di Sant'Anna dei Lombardi in the right-hand corner. Walk down the slope and cross Via Monteoliveto, and then walk up Calata Trinità Maggiore into the busy Piazza del Gesù Nuovo. There are plenty of cafés in the piazza for some well-earned refreshment.

INFORMATION

Distance 2km (1.2 miles)
Time 1.5 hours
Start point Piazza del Plebiscito
🚇 C25, R3
End point Piazza del Gesù Nuovo
🚇 E1, R4

The statue of Ferdinand I in the peaceful and airy Piazza del Plebiscito

Naples by Night

The solid bulk of the Castel Nuovo at night

JAZZ

The foremost jazz club in the city is Otto Jazz (✉ Piazzetta Cariati 24 ☎ 081 666 262), where internationally renowned players can be heard. Another jazz-oriented club is Murat (✉ Via Vincenzo Bellini 8 ☎ 081 544 5919), and you can also catch good jazz occasionally at Lontano da Dove (✉ Via Vincenzo Bellini 3 ☎ 081 549 4304) and Bourbon Street (✉ Via Vincenzo Bellini 52 ☎ 328 068 7221). Up in Vomero, local jazz musicians play at Around Midnight (✉ Via Bonito 32A ☎ 081 558 2834). One of the most well-known local jazz musicians is Daniel Sepe, who mixes modern jazz with more traditional Italian music. You may be lucky enough to catch him at one of these venues.

There is no excuse for a quiet night in while visiting Naples, as there is enough variety of entertainment to suit everyone. Most expensive, but highly rewarding, would be a visit to the opera at Teatro San Carlo. Performances are invariably excellent, although it is almost as much fun to watch the audience. Other musical events take place all through the summer, with concerts in churches and other venues, where everything from early music to popular classics is performed.

Lovers of pop and rock music are equally well catered to, with several clubs and dance bars, many of them close to the student areas of Centro Storico. The bigger clubs, however, tend to be out of town in Posillipo, or even further out. The big event is the *Neapolis* festival in Bagnoli at the end of July.

Playhouses are plentiful, but most performances are in Italian. There is a lively strand of experimental drama in the city but, again, it may be difficult to follow. Cinemas also generally show films in, or dubbed into, Italian.

A relaxing way to spend the evening is to sit with a drink in one of the many bars. Some play music and have dancing later in the evening. Others serve food and drink until quite late. Piazza Bellini is one of the most attractive areas in the evening, with several bars, cafés and restaurants full of lively, chattering crowds. The evening ritual of the *passegiata* is enjoyed here, where local people stroll up and down, talking and meeting friends.

NAPLES'
top 25 sights

The sights are shown on the maps on the inside front cover and inside back cover, numbered **1**–**25** across the city

Villa la Floridiana

This refined neoclassical villa, built for a royal mistress and set in peaceful parkland on the hill in Vomero, makes an entirely appropriate setting for a huge collection of exquisite porcelain.

Palace for a duchess Nine months after his first wife died, King Ferdinand I of Bourbon married his mistress, the Duchess of Floridia. In 1817, he built for her this neoclassical villa, which sits in a beautiful park with superb sea views. It was purchased by the state in 1919 and has become the home of the Duca di Martina Museum of Ceramics. The duke was a fanatical collector, and toured all over Europe gathering up porcelain, ceramics and other objets d'art. The central room in the house has a notable ceiling, decorated in Capodimonte style and depicting mythological creatures. The other rooms are also grand, but are given over to display cases.

Majolica and porcelain The collection runs to around 700 pieces, most of them exquisitely beautiful. The ground floor holds the most valuable collection of majolica, which includes items from Moorish Spain and some beautiful medicine jars from the Renaissance period from Gubbio and Faenza. Also on this floor are luminous items of Venetian glass together with English and Bohemian crystal. Particularly valuable are the Limoges enamels from the 15th and 16th centuries. There are some exquisite displays of porcelain on the first floor, much of it German Meissen and French Sèvres, but also including some Italian works. Capodimonte pieces are in the ballroom, along with other works produced in Naples. The basement rooms contain a huge collection of Chinese and Japanese items, with some lovely blue and white vases.

Castel Sant'Elmo

Prisoners down the ages must have cursed this solid citadel, but high-quality restoration has revealed other aspects of its history to balance the picture.

Medieval stronghold There has been a castle on St. Erasmus (shortened to Sant'Elmo) Hill since 1275, before which there was a small church. King Robert of Anjou enlarged it in 1329, using a famous architect of the time, Tino di Camaino, who was also working on the Certosa (▶ 28) next door. It was damaged by the earthquake in 1456 and parts of the walls and towers collapsed. Between 1537 and 1547 it was rebuilt by the viceroy Don Pedro de Toledo as part of a project to defend Naples by using a ring of castles, during which period it acquired its distinctive shape of a six-pointed star, which was highly unusual at the time.

Explosions and restoration A church was built in the parade ground, and the coat of arms of Don Pedro de Toledo can be seen in the sacristy. A rare disaster struck in 1587 when the ammunition store was hit by lightning, killing many people and damaging the church and much of the castle. Restoration began more than ten years later, but the castle's era as a stern fortress was over. From this point it was primarily used as a prison until the mid-1970s, housing the leaders of the Neapolitan revolution in 1799, and many people involved in the *Risorgimento*, the struggle for Italian unification, in 1860. Today, restoration work has uncovered many of the original walkways, and a large auditorium has been created where concerts, plays and exhibitions are held. Perhaps the most rewarding part of a visit here is the outstanding view that can be enjoyed from the ramparts.

HIGHLIGHTS

- Views of the city from the ramparts
- Arms of Hapsburg Emperor Charles V over entrance portal
- Unusual six-pointed star layout
- Superb restoration of the auditorium

INFORMATION

- ✚ C3
- ✉ Via Tito Angelini 20
- ☎ 081 558 7708
- 🕐 Tue–Sun 8.30–7.30; closed Mon and 1 Jan, Good Fri, 1 May, 25 Dec
- 🍴 Cafés (€€) in Piazza Vanvitelli
- 🚋 Vanvitelli, Funicolare Piazza Fuga, Funicolare Via Morghen
- 🚌 181, C28, C30, C31, C32
- ♿ Few
- 💶 Moderate; combined ticket with Certosa di San Martino (▶ 28)
- ↔ Certosa di San Martino (▶ 28), Villa La Floridiana (▶ 26)
- ❓ Open-air films in the courtyard in summer

Naples from the citadel of Castel Sant'Elmo

27

Certosa di San Martino

INFORMATION

- C3
- Piazza San Martino 8
- 081 558 6408
- Tue–Sat 8.30–7.30, Sun 9–7.30; closed Mon and 1 Jan, Good Fri, 1 May, 25 Dec
- Cafés (€€) in Piazza Vanvitelli
- Vanvitelli, Funicolare Piazza Fuga, Funicolare Via Morghen
- 181, C28, C30, C31, C32
- Few
- Moderate; combined ticket with Castel Sant'Elmo
- Castel Sant'Elmo (► 27), Villa la Floridiana (► 26)

One of the highlights of a visit to Naples must be this glorious place, with its superb views over the city, and its quite extraordinary collection of paintings and other works of art.

Monastic wealth Overlooking the city and with a beautiful setting, this remarkable monastery is filled with sumptuous works of art. *Certosa* means charterhouse, and it was founded by the Carthusians in 1325 around the same time as Castel Sant'Elmo (► 27) next door. It gradually accumulated many priceless treasures related to Naples and the surrounding area. The monastery was dissolved by the French in 1806, and it fell into disrepair until it was restored after World War II. The baroque church is rich with Neapolitan paintings by masters such as Fanzago, Stanzione and Ribera. Leading from the church is the peaceful Clerk's Cloister and, beyond that, is the charming Great Cloister. In one corner is the monks' graveyard, whose balustrade is ornamented with skulls.

Riches of the museum The restoration of the Prior's Quarters provides a graphic insight into the richness of the monks' way of life, with magnificent paintings, sculpture, and furniture. Just below the apartments is the small, tranquil garden used by the prior. Particularly interesting is the art gallery in the rooms around the sides of the Great Cloister, where there are several scenes of Naples as it used to be. In one of the rooms is a superbly detailed model of the Certosa and the Castel Sant'Elmo. Among the many other attractions is a collection of *presepi* (Christmas crèches), which includes one huge example with hundreds of animals, shepherds and individual figures. A museum demonstrates the heritage of Neapolitan drama and song.

Catacombe San Gennaro

Very important mosaics and frescoes line the walls of these famous catacombs dedicated to the city's patron saint. The catacombs are somewhat dilapidated, but have been sought out by pilgrims and tourists for centuries.

San Gennaro The patron saint of Naples, San Gennaro, was born in the third century AD in either Naples or in Benevento, but only a little is known of his life. Arrested by the Roman emperor Diocletian on suspicion of being a Christian, he miraculously survived being thrown head first into a furnace, and also being fed to the lions, but was finally executed in AD305. His blood was collected in some glass vials, which are now in the Duomo, and it is said to turn bright red and bubble on his feast day, 19 September. Local citizens brought his body back to the city, and initially buried it in these catacombs, although it was subsequently moved to the Duomo. Regrettably, San Gennaro was demoted by the Pope in the 1960s, but Naples still continues to worship him.

Frescoes and tombs The catacombs date from the second century, when they are thought to have held the tomb of a pagan aristocrat. Sant'Agrippino was buried here, but they became a place of pilgrimage after San Gennaro's body arrived. Neapolitan bishops were buried here right up until the 11th century. The site is on two levels and is quite extensive. The upper floor has some frescoes dating from the second to the tenth centuries, one of which represents San Gennaro. The lower level has the chapel of Sant'Agrippino and a baptistery.

HIGHLIGHTS

- Pleasant garden by the entrance with views over Sanità
- Second-century frescoes
- Image of San Gennaro
- Baptismal font dating from eighth century
- Bishop's Crypt

INFORMATION

- ✚ D1
- ✉ Via Capodimonte 16
- ☎ 081 741 1071
- 🕐 Daily tours 9.30, 10.15, 11, 11.45
- 🚌 24, R4
- ♿ None
- 💶 Moderate
- ↔ Museo di Capodimonte (► 37), Osservatorio Astronomico (► 53)
- ❓ The approach is by the side of Chiesa della Madre del Buon Consiglio

Above and below: Leaf-form mosaic in catacombs

29

Castel dell'Ovo

Infused with venerable myths and tales of days long gone, this ancient castle sits solidly, looking out into the Bay of Naples yet reflecting the history of the city behind it.

Virgil's spell The strange name of this castle (Castle of the Egg) is allegedly linked to the poet Virgil, who lived in Naples in the first century BC, when the city was flourishing under the Roman Empire. He cast a spell on a magic egg buried in the castle, whereby so long as the egg remained unbroken, the city and the castle were safe.

Doughty fortress In Roman times, the castle was a pleasure palace for the patrician Lucullus, but its origins lie further back in time with the Greeks, who founded Parthenope around 800BC. When the Normans conquered the city in 1139 it was turned into a fortress and royal residence. Frederick II kept the crown jewels here in the 13th century. During Spanish rule in the 15th century, it was refortified, but a century later it was almost destroyed in a siege. Its present appearance is the result of the subsequent rebuilding (started in 1503), but after that it fell into a decline and at one time (in the 19th century) was almost demolished, before restoration work was begun in the 1970s.

The castle today It has been superbly restored, and is now used for exhibitions and conferences. The sloping ramp leads to walkways that have wonderful views across the bay. A few cannons remain on the gun emplacements. Some of the restored rooms are gigantic, and it is also possible to see tunnels in the rock (probably built by successive prisoners). The area around the castle, Borgo Marinaro, is full of bars and restaurants, and is very lively on summer evenings.

The Lungomare

Neapolitans and visitors alike enjoy the walk of 3km (almost 2 miles) by the sea away from the bustle of the Centro Storico to the relaxed setting of a mini seaside resort.

Santa Maria The path along the waterfront from Santa Lucia to Mergellina is known to the locals as the Lungomare. It is a very pleasant walk (➤ 22) with views of Vesuvio and of the city as you go along. At one time, the nearest road to the coast was Via Santa Lucia, but in the 19th century, the intervening land was reclaimed, and Via Nazario Sauro and Via Partenope were built. The hill behind Via Santa Lucia is Pizzofalcone, the hill on which Neapolis was founded by the Greeks in the fifth century BC.

Villa Comunale Heading towards Piazza Vittoria, where dozens of buses congregate, the road is bordered by the Villa Comunale, a green lung for the city, with plenty of space in which to walk and play. The park was designed by Vanvitelli and finished in 1781, although it was enlarged in the 19th century. It has statues, fountains and an impressive bandstand—all the features of a respectable public park. Behind it lies the district of Chiaia, a very smart area of the city with fashionable stores and elegant houses.

Mergellina The park ends at Piazza della Repubblica, which marks the start of Mergellina. It is a fishing and yachting centre, and is also the terminal for boats to Ischia, Capri and Sorrento. Lining the waterfront are a number of chalets which serve ice cream and snacks. Some years ago these were among the most fashionable places in Naples, but they are a little run down now. The ice cream, however, is as good as ever.

HIGHLIGHTS

● Smart hotels and restaurants of Santa Lucia
● Wonderful views across the bay
● Villa Comunale and its peaceful walks
● Fishermen's huts at Mergellina
● Ice cream while gazing at the sea

INFORMATION

✚ B4
✉ Via Partenope, Via Francesco Caracciolo
🍴 Cafés (€) in Santa Lucia and Mergellina
🚇 Mergellina
🚌 140, C9, C10, C24, C25, E5, R3
♿ Good
🔁 Castel dell'Ovo (➤ 30), Stazione Zoologica (➤ 53), Museo Villa Pignatelli (➤ 52), Villa Comunale (➤ 56), Porticciolo di Mergellina (➤ 56), Chiesa di Santa Maria del Parto (➤ 55), Parco Virgiliano (➤ 56)

31

Piazza del Plebiscito

- Grand, open space, one of the finest piazzas in Italy
- Caffè Gambrinus, on the far side, with its art nouveau interior
- Façade of Palazzo Reale, designed by Vanvitelli, facing the piazza
- Statues of Neapolitan kings on Palazzo Reale façade

INFORMATION

- D3
- Caffè Gambrinus (€€)
- Funicolare Augusteo
- 24, C22, C82, R2, R3
- Good
- Palazzo Reale (➤ 36), Teatro San Carlo (➤ 35), Castel Nuovo (➤ 41), Galleria Umberto I (➤ 34)

This huge area, great for strolling in, admiring the architecture all around, or for keeping out of the sun under the colonnade, is a focal point in the city and is always full of life.

Until the early part of the 19th century, the area occupied by the Piazza del Plebiscito was a mess. The ruler at the time, Napoleon's brother-in-law Joachim Murat, built a large piazza for military parades and civil ceremonies (started in 1809). Before it could be finished, however, the French were driven out of Naples and the Bourbons were reinstated. In 1815, Ferdinand of Bourbon carried on with the work and commissioned the stately church of San Francesco di Paola, which faces across to the Palazzo Reale. It is a very grand church, on the model of Rome's Pantheon, but rather soulless. The two equestrian statues are of Charles III and Ferdinand I.

The piazza suffered during World War II, and in the post-war years was used primarily for car and bus parking. However, many areas, including the piazza, were smartened up in readiness for the G7 summit, held in Naples in 1994. Now it is one of the finest open spaces in the city, with plenty of room to stroll and enjoy the elegant surroundings. The central area is usually occupied by a large piece of modern art, and the whole airy piazza is ideal for open-air concerts and other festivities.

One side is occupied by the Palazzo Reale, with its array of statues in niches facing the piazza. They include important figures from the city's history, such as Joachim Murat, who created the original scheme, and Victor Emmanuel II of Savoy, the first king of the united Italian state.

Santa Maria della Sanità

The church itself is rather formal; the real interest lies underneath it in the fifth-century catacombs with their fragments of frescoes and the strange burial methods of more recent times.

Domed church Sanità is a working-class district below the road connecting Museo di Capodimonte to the city. At its heart lies this church, also known as San Vincenzo (as it houses a statue of San Vincent). It was built in 1613, and is a very spacious church, designed on the pattern of a Greek cross. The huge central dome is supported by 24 columns, and has 12 smaller domes around it. Among its paintings is one by Giordano. There is also an early Christian stone pulpit where, tradition has it, pregnant women can sit to gain protection against losing their babies. The main altar is unusual in that it can be raised up. It is situated in a chapel in front of the entrance to the catacombs, and when it is raised the congregation can see this entrance.

Catacombs of San Gaudioso The catacombs below the church have acquired their fame from the burial there of San Gaudioso. He was an African bishop from the fifth century AD who was stripped of all of his belongings and set adrift in an old boat, which fortuitously landed at Naples. He set up a monastery and died around AD452. His burial place here became a shrine, and there are still traces of frescoes dating back to the fifth century AD. The catacombs continued to be used as a cemetery, and there are some gruesome remains from the 17th century, when the skulls were set into the wall and the outlines of the skeletons were drawn below them. The catacombs can be visited on guided tours.

HIGHLIGHTS

- Impressive central dome in church
- Ingenious rising altar
- Catacombs of San Gaudioso
- Frescoes from fifth century AD
- Starting point for exploring Sanità district

INFORMATION

www.cib.na.cnr.it/ntnp.html
- D1
- Via Sanità 124
- 081 544 1305
- Mon–Sat 8.30–12.30, Sun 8.30–1.30; tours daily 9.30, 10.15, 11, 11.45, 12.30 (Sat also 5.10, 5.50, 6.30)
- Piazza Cavour, Museo
- 47, 182, C51, C52, C64, C83
- None
- Moderate
- Museo di Capodimonte (➤ 37), Museo Archeologico Nazionale (➤ 38), Catacombe San Gennaro (➤ 29)
- Telephone ahead for English-speaking guide

33

Galleria Umberto I

HIGHLIGHTS

- Glass-domed roof
- Zodiac mosaic on marble floor
- Superb engineering
- Tasty *sfogliatelle* from one of the cafés

INFORMATION

- D3
- Via San Carlo
- Arcade: open permanently; shops 9–1, 4–7; closed Sun
- Cafés (€–€€) in the Galleria and in Piazza Trieste e Trento
- Funicolare Augusteo
- 24, C22, C82, R2, R3
- Good
- Free
- Teatro San Carlo (► 35), Palazzo Reale (► 36), Piazza del Plebiscito (► 32)

This stylish gallery must have been an arresting sight at the turn of the 20th century, with the light from its huge glass roof shining down on the city's élite.

Early shopping mall This most impressive glass-and steel-domed shopping gallery had its hey-day in the early part of the 20th century, when fashionable society came here to shop, to see and be seen, and to visit the local opera house. Today it is much quieter, home to smart clothes shops and jewellers, and some welcome cafés. It is also haunted by bootleg CD and handbag sellers. At Christmas time, the area really comes to life with a giant illuminated *presepe* (Christmas crèche). It has always been a matter of contention between Naples and Milan as to which city had the smarter gallery, and although it is not as big as Milan's Galleria Vittorio Emanuele II, Galleria Umberto I is probably the more imposing architecturally.

Engineering marvel It was built in 1890 as part of a project to revitalize the city after the devastating cholera outbreak of 1884. All the slums in the Santa Brigida area were demolished and the *galleria* was built in their place, leading off the then fashionable Via Toledo, and facing across from the prestigious Teatro San Carlo. It was seen as a symbol of the modernization of the city. The architect was Antonio Curri, following a design by Emanuele Rocca. Above a central mosaic paving of the zodiac on the marble floor below, the dome, by Paolo Boubée, is 57m (188ft) high. The colonnades are ornamented with allegorical Greco-Roman sculptures and faced with polychrome marble. The overall effect is of a confident, turn-of-the-century building, now with a slightly faded grandeur.

Teatro San Carlo

Once the world's most important opera house, this famous locale still attracts today's leading artistes. Superb performances in such a gorgeous building make for vivid memories.

A night at the opera For many people, one of the highlights of the social calendar is a visit to this famous opera house. The Neapolitan audience is extremely discerning, and even Caruso was hissed here. Tickets go quickly, but for any music lover an evening at Teatro San Carlo will be a must. For those who merely want to see the sumptuous interior, guided tours take place when work schedules permit.

Bourbon masterpiece The opera house is one of the oldest in the world. It was built in 1737, after only 300 days' work, at the behest of director and impresario Angelo Carasale and opened on the saint's day of Bourbon King Charles III. The opulent interior was covered in gold, silver and blue (to reflect the Bourbon royal household), and it became one of the most important venues in Europe. Sadly, a fire caused serious damage in 1816, but it was restored within nine months. Today, the Teatro has 184 boxes, arranged in six tiers, and a royal box that seats 15. The glorious painting on the ceiling is of Giuseppe Cammarano's Apollo introducing the greatest poets in the world to the goddess Minerva.

Musical heritage Famous composers have had their works premièred here, including Rossini, who was conductor and composer here from 1815 to 1822, with his operas *Mosè in Egitto* and *La Donna del Lago*. Donizetti's *Lucia di Lammermoor* also had its world première in the Teatro. Today it is still a magnet for all the leading performers in the opera world.

HIGHLIGHTS

- Lavish royal box
- Beautiful ceiling painting
- Elaborate interior
- Performances to remember

INFORMATION

www.teatrosancarlo.it
- D3
- Via San Carlo 98/F
- 081 400 300
- Opera season Mon–Fri 10–3.30, Nov–Jun; guided tours all year, times vary according to work schedules
- Cafés (€–€€) in the Galleria Umberto I and in Piazza Trieste e Trento
- Funicolare Augusteo
- 24, C22, C82, R2, R3
- Few
- Tickets expensive; guided tours moderate
- Galleria Umberto I (► 34), Palazzo Reale (► 36), Piazza del Plebiscito (► 32)
- The resident ballet company is also one of the oldest in Italy

35

Palazzo Reale

INFORMATION

- ✚ D3
- ✉ Piazza del Plebiscito 1
- ☎ 081 794 4053/081 794 4021
- 🕐 Thu–Tue 9–8; closed Wed, 1 Jan, 1 May, 25 Dec
- 🍴 Cafés (€–€€) in Piazza Trieste e Trento
- 🚠 Funicolare Augusteo
- 🚌 24, C22, C82, R2, R3
- ♿ Few
- 💶 Moderate
- 🔁 Castel Nuovo (➤ 41), Galleria Umberto I (➤ 34), Piazza del Plebiscito (➤ 32)
- ❓ Look out for ticket office to the left of main entrance

Built to receive Philip III of Spain (who never came), the huge royal palace was the seat of power in Naples for three centuries, and held one of the most important courts in Europe.

Origins Enter the palace through the majestic 16th-century façade facing Piazza del Plebiscito, but first admire the eight statues of Italian kings set in niches. It is an enormous building (there are 30 rooms in the Royal Apartments alone), packed with interest.

Royal Apartments To enter the Royal Apartments climb the elaborate marble staircase, built in 1651—50 years after work started on the palace. The original style was lavish Bourbon, but successive rulers modified the decoration and expanded the building. The present rooms display a variety of taste from the 17th to the 19th centuries, and contain a fascinating collection of paintings and tapestries. Of particular note are the Throne Room (Room 6) with its massive throne, the impressive collection of clocks in the Flemish Hall (Room 13), the Sala del Gran Capitano (Room 13) with its marvellous ceiling frescoes, and the huge Sala di Ercole (Room 22) lined with tapestries. Don't miss Room 23, with its clever rotating lectern.

Priceless treasures One of the most charming parts of the palace is the Teatrino di Corte (at the top of the main staircase), built in 1768 and restored after damage in World War II. It is highly ornate and has unusual papier mâché statues. Also take time to look at the gilded Cappella Palatina where the giant *presepe* (crèche) is kept and the Biblioteca Nazionale Vittorio Emanuele III (the largest library in southern Italy), then go outside to see the peaceful small garden.

Museo di Capodimonte

What better way to appreciate some of the best art in Italy than to come up to this palace on the hill, with its panoramic views, and study the great masters on display here.

Hunting lodge to art gallery Bourbon King Charles III had this grand palace built in 1738, originally only to be a hunting lodge, but expanded to house the superb art collection he inherited from his mother, Elizabeth Farnese. Through many additions and changes, it has now become one of the most important art collections in Italy, and is well organized and structured.

Mezzanine floor The museum's priceless collection of drawings and prints (around 25,000) is housed here, including some cartoons by Michelangelo for the Paolina Chapel in Rome, and by Raphael for a room in the Vatican.

First floor Among the many treasures in the Farnese Gallery are pictures by Bellini, Breughel the Elder, Titian, Masaccio, El Greco, Carracci and Parmigianino. The earliest pieces in the collection date from 1290 and continue to the 16th century. Also on this floor, together with the rest of the Royal Apartments, is the porcelain parlour of Maria Amalia, which has thousands of pieces of Capodimonte porcelain.

Second floor In addition to the treasures from the collection of Neapolitan artists, there are two remarkable paintings that cannot be missed here—Titian's wonderful *Annunciation*, and Caravaggio's powerful *Flagellation of Christ*.

Third floor Contemporary art has pride of place on this floor—particularly striking is Andy Warhol's *Vesuvius*.

HIGHLIGHTS

- Caravaggio's *Flagellation of Christ*
- Titian's *Danaë*
- Parmigianino's hypnotic *Antea*
- Maria Amalia's Porcelain Parlour
- Andy Warhol's *Vesuvius*
- Drawings and prints collection

INFORMATION

- ✚ D1
- ✉ Via di Maiano 1
- ☎ 081 749 9111
- 🕐 Tue–Sun 8.30–7.30; closed Mon, 1 Jan, 25 Dec
- 🍴 Café on ground floor
- 🚌 24, 137, 178, C66, R4
- ♿ Good
- 💶 Expensive; park free
- 🔗 Catacombe San Gennaro (➤ 29), Osservatorio Astronomico (➤ 53), Santa Maria della Sanità (➤ 33)
- ❓ Audio tours in main languages

Museo Archeologico Nazionale

HIGHLIGHTS

- Model of Pompei (Room 96)
- Blue Vase (Room 81)
- Battle of Alexander mosaic (Room 61)
- Farnese Hercules (Room 12)
- Sundial room
- Temple of Isis (Room 83)

INFORMATION

- ➕ D2
- ✉ Piazza Museo 19
- ☎ 081 440 166
- ⏰ Wed–Mon 9–8; closed Tue, 1 Jan, 1 May, 25 Dec
- Ⓜ Museo, Piazzo Cavour
- 🚌 24, 47, 137, 178, 201, CS, E1, R4
- ♿ Good
- 🍴 Expensive
- ↔ Piazza Bellini (➤ 39), Piazza Dante (➤ 58), Santa Maria della Sanità (➤ 33), San Paolo Maggiore (➤ 54)
- ❓ Audio guides available; tours only to Gabinetto Segreto

A visit to this comprehensive and well-laid-out museum, which is packed with priceless treasures and gorgeous objects, will help the visitor to understand the ruins at Pompei.

World-class museum One of the most important archaeological museums in the world, this is a spectacular collection of finds, predominantly from southern Italy. It is housed in the former university building, and the displays are clear and modern. The museum was set up by Charles III at about the same time as Capodimonte, and originally contained all the Farnese collection. It still has the sculptures and archaeological finds.

Farnese collection Huge statues of Hercules, Flora, and the Farnese Bull are Roman copies of Greek originals, and dominate the hall they occupy. There are also other works that have been found near Vesuvio.

Egyptian collection Down in the basement, this group of objects shows the close links between the Roman civilization and Egypt. The Egyptian collection includes beautiful statues, and also an embalmed crocodile, a sacred creature in ancient Egypt.

Pompei and Ercolano The museum's fame rests, to a large extent, on its fabulous finds from these sites, and therefore any visit to either of them should be preceded by some time spent here to view the wealth of material unearthed. Among the many displays are some impressive mosaics, including a charming one with cat and ducks, and some beautiful glassware, pottery and silver, as well as erotic pictures and sculptures from Pompei, in the Gabinetto Segreto.

Piazza Bellini

One of the most fashionable piazzas in Naples, the Piazza Bellini is always thronged with people and surrounded by excellent cafés and restaurants as well as unusual and historic buildings.

Greek origins Popular with locals and visitors alike, this is a lively piazza at any time, with students milling about, intellectuals arguing in the cafés, and families walking up and down. It used to lie just outside the old city walls until the 16th century, and excavations have revealed evidence of the old walls of the original Greek city of Neapolis (a new city south of Parthenope). These walls are of regular shapes of tufa stone and can be seen in the middle of the piazza, under the gaze of the statue of the composer Vincenzo Bellini. Neapolis was founded by the Greeks in 470BC, and survived until 326BC, when the Romans took it after besieging the city for two years.

Surrounding buildings Around the piazza are some interesting buildings. In the northwest corner is Palazzo Firrao, built in the 17th century for the Prince of Sant'Agata. It has an unusual façade made up of the busts of the Spanish kings and royal families who ruled Naples at this time. At the northern end is the monastery of Sant'Antonio delle Monache a Port Alba, which dates from 1564. When it was enlarged in 1637, it incorporated the Palazzo Conca. The present façade was built in the 18th century, with an imposing double flight of steps. Around the corner from the piazza is the Teatro Bellini, considered by many to be the most beautiful such building in the city. It was built in 1877 and opened to Vincenzo Bellini's opera *The Puritans and the Knights*. It is one of the major *teatris* in the city and puts on opera, ballet and musical shows as well as plays.

HIGHLIGHTS

- Statue of Vincenzo Bellini
- Remains of Greek walls
- Churches and palaces round the piazza
- Lively relaxed atmosphere

INFORMATION

- D2
- Piazza Bellini
- Intra Moenia (€€), Piazza Bellini 70
- Dante
- 201, C57, E1, R1, R4
- Good
- Museo Archeologico Nazionale (➤ 38), Piazza Dante (➤ 58), San Domenico Maggiore (➤ 44), Gesù Nuovo (➤ 40)

Gesù Nuovo

From the outside, this church looks rather grim with its grey ashlar façade. But venture inside, and it is full of baroque riches, Neapolitan art and memories of a modern saint.

HIGHLIGHTS

- Renaissance entrance
- Solimena's fresco on the inner façade
- Chapel of St. Ignatius
- Chapel of Giuseppe Moscati
- Barrel-vaulted ceiling

INFORMATION

- D2
- Piazza del Gesù Nuovo 2
- 081 551 8613
- Daily 7–1, 4.30–7
- Caffè Novecento (➤ 68), Patisserie Scaturchio (➤ 70)
- Dante
- E1, R1, R4
- Good
- Free
- Piazza Bellini (➤ 39), Santa Chiara (➤ 42), San Domenico Maggiore (➤ 44), Piazza Dante (➤ 58)

Original palace Before it was sold to the Jesuits in 1548, this was the Palazzo Sanseverino di Salerno, which was built in 1470. The original gateway to the old palace is preserved in the entrance portal. The rather bleak, grey, diamond-shaped stones that form the exterior wall give no hint of the riches inside.

Ornate frescoes The church's ornate baroque interior is covered with marble, frescoes and statues. The central dome has been rebuilt a number of times (most recently in the 19th century) and the rest of the church adopts a Greek cross plan. Over the last three centuries, almost every important artist in Naples has contributed to the decoration. Cosimo Fanzago, a highly prolific Neapolitan artist, made the splendid statues of *David* and *Jeremiah* in the Chapel of St. Ignatius. Francesco Solimena painted the huge fresco on the inner façade in 1725. Another artist from the city, Luca Giordano, produced the paintings in the chapel of San Francesco Saverio.

Modern saint A more recent saint is Giuseppe Moscati, a local doctor who dedicated himself to looking after the city's poor, although he was academically gifted and an active researcher. He believed there was a close link between medicine and religion, and tried to unite the two disciplines. He was highly regarded by the people, but died in 1927 at the early age of 47. The populace pressed for his canonization in 1987, and he is commemorated in the second chapel on the right in the church.

Castel Nuovo

Not only does the solid bulk of this fortress make it a major landmark in the city, it is also the focal point of much of Naples' turbulent history through the centuries.

Angevin castle The locals know it as *Maschio Angioino* (keep of the Angevin kings), although its present appearance is mainly due to the work of Alfonso of Aragon, who became king of Naples and Sicily. He rebuilt the 13th-century Angevin castle in 1443. The original construction was designed to replace the defensive functions of Castel dell'Ovo and Castel Capuano. Alfonso faced the five solid towers with *piperno*, a very hard material composed of volcanic lava ash mixed with stone and seawater. The entrance is through the beautiful Arco di Trionfo, where a relief celebrates Alfonso's entry into the city. Across the courtyard, the Cappella Palatina is all that remains of the original 13th-century castle. True, the chapel has been given a Renaissance doorway, but inside it is austere and refined. It was originally decorated with frescoes by Giotto, but sadly all but a few traces were lost in the 1456 earthquake. (There are some great views of the bay to be enjoyed from the castle terrace.)

Spanish intrigue In dramatic contrast, the Sala dei Baroni (Baronial Hall) shows strong Spanish influence, especially in its star-shaped ceiling. Its name comes from a treacherous episode when Alfonso's son, Ferrante, pretended to make a truce with some rebel barons, arranged a marriage between his niece and the chief rebel, and then arrested all the barons at the wedding breakfast. The first and second floors house the Museo Civico (Civic Museum), which has a collection of 19th-century Neapolitan paintings.

HIGHLIGHTS

- ● Arco di Trionfo
- ● Cappella Palatina
- ● Sala dei Baroni
- ● Roman remains in Sala dell'Armeria

INFORMATION

- ✚ D3
- ✉ Piazza Municipio
- ☎ 081 795 5877
- 🕐 Mon–Sat 9–7, Sun 9–2
- 🍴 Cafés (€) in Galleria Umberto I and in Piazza Trieste e Trento
- Ⓖ Funicolare Augusteo
- 🚌 C25, C82, E3, R2, R3, R4
- ♿ Good
- Ⓜ Moderate
- ↔ Palazzo Reale (➤ 36), Galleria Umberto I (➤ 34), Teatro San Carlo (➤ 35)

41

Santa Chiara

INFORMATION

www.oltreilchiostro.org

+ D3

⊠ Via Benedetto Croce, Via Santa Chiara 49

☎ 081 552 6209

🕐 Church: daily 7–12.30, 4–7; cloister and museum: Mon–Sat 9.30–1, 2.30–5.30, Sun 9.30–1

🍴 Scaturchio (€) ⊠ Piazza San Domenico Maggiore 19

🚇 Dante

🚌 201, C57, E1, R1, R4

♿ Few

💲 Moderate

↔ Gesù Nuovo (▶ 40), San Domenico Maggiore (▶ 44), Piazza Dante (▶ 58), Piazza Bellini (▶ 39)

❓ Occasional concerts are held here

Simplicity and peace emanate from this beautiful church, with its royal connections and enchanting cloisters. Rising from the ashes of war, it is one of the most important city attractions.

Royal church In the hustle and bustle of Spaccanapoli, this beautiful church is an oasis of serenity. It is a large complex and worth making time for. Its origins lie in the 14th century when Robert of Anjou made it a royal church. His wife, Sancia, added a convent for the Clarissa Sisters (known as the Poor Clares because of their vow of poverty). The church houses the tomb of King Robert (died 1343) as well as several other royal notables, including Philip of Bourbon (died 1777). As a result of all of this royal patronage, during the 18th century the church became one of the most elaborately decorated, but a bomb in 1943 caused a disastrous fire and much destruction. Restoration gave the opportunity to get back to the simple, original Gothic style, which is so impressive today. Some parts of the original church were rescued, including the rose window and the wooden crucifix on the main altar. A separate bell tower, to the left of the church, still has its own base.

Tranquil cloisters At the back of the church are the 14th-century cloisters, which are probably the most beautiful in Italy. Yellow and green majolica tiles cover the pillars which run across the middle of the courtyard between the orange trees, while the seats round the edge (not to be sat on) have delightful pictures of pastoral scenes. This peaceful spot offers a respite from the strains of sightseeing. To one side of the cloisters is the small museum, which has some sculptures from the damaged church, and also some traces of the Roman baths.

Spaccanapoli

The historic heart of Naples encapsulates all the popular images of this lively city, with its excitable characters, delicious food and its wealth of art and architecture.

Roman origins Appearing to split Naples in two (the meaning of its name), Spaccanapoli follows the path of the old Roman road, *decamanus inferior*. There were two other Roman roads through the city: *decamanus maior* (Via dei Tribunali) and *decamanus superior* (Via dell'Anticaglia). One of the liveliest areas in Naples, it is filled with churches, palaces, shops, restaurants, stalls and bars.

Street of palaces There are so many things to see here that it is impossible to do justice to them all, but some are described in this book: Gesù Nuovo (▶ 40), Santa Chiara (▶ 42), San Domenico Maggiore (▶ 44) and Sant'Angelo a Nilo (▶ 54). Other important buildings (not open) to look out for in Via Benedetto Croce are the 14th-century Palazzo Filomarino (No. 12), where the 20th-century philosopher Benedetto Croce lived and died; Palazzo Venezia (No. 19), where the Venetian ambassador lived while Venice was a republic; and Palazzo Carafo della Spina (No. 45), which has some tall 16th-century doors, as well as two marble lions. Further along the street becomes Via San Biagio dei Librai, where there are some more fine buildings such as Palazzo Carafa Santangelo (No. 121), and Monte di Pietà (No. 114).

Lively squares There is more than wonderful architecture to this street, however. The two main piazzas, Gesù Nuovo and San Domenico, throb with life at all hours. Another good spot is Piazzetta Nilo, with its famous statue of the deified god, Nile, known as *The Body of Naples*.

HIGHLIGHTS

- Santa Chiara (▶ 42)
- Piazza San Domenico
- Piazzetta Nilo
- Cakes from Scaturchio's

INFORMATION

- E2
- Via Benedetto Croce, Via San Biago ai Librai, Via Vicaria Vecchia
- Many good restaurants and cafés along these streets
- Dante
- 201, C57, E1, R1, R4
- Few
- Cappella Sansevero (▶ 45), San Lorenzo Maggiore (▶ 47), Duomo (▶ 48)
- There are information signposts for the principal monuments along the itinerary of the 'museo aperto' (open museum)

43

San Domenico Maggiore

In one of the liveliest piazzas in the city, this large church, which has been both a monastery and a university department, has many beautiful works of art.

Seat of learning Dominican monks in the 13th century had this church and monastery generously built for them in 1238 by Charles I. It became the main department of theology for Naples university, and Thomas Aquinas lived and taught here for a while. It is said that an icon near the altar whispered temptations to him, but he resisted. One of the chapels is dedicated to him.

Changing fortunes Enter the church from Vico San Domenico, past the door of San Michele Archangelo a Morfisa, which formed the basis for this church. The vast interior is rather like a cathedral and it has one of the best collections of art of any church in the city. It has suffered many changes through the years, being badly damaged by fire in 1506, and being completely transformed into a neo-Gothic style in the 19th century. The result is a feast for the eyes, and a mixture of periods in art.

Wealth of art One of its most famous paintings, *Flagellation of Christ* by Caravaggio, is now in the Museo di Capodimonte (► 37), but a copy is kept here. Raphael painted his *Madonna del Pesce* for one of the chapels, but that painting is now in the Madrid Prado. Giotto's pupil, Pietro Cavallini, produced the 14th-century frescoes in the second chapel on the right. Particularly impressive is the painted ceiling in the sacristy, *Triumph of Faith over Heresy* by the Neapolitan artist Francesco Solimena. The church also contains dozens of tombs of the sovereigns and aristocrats of the Aragonese court.

Cappella Sansevero

This little private chapel contains some of the most extraordinary and bizarre sculptures to be found anywhere in the city. No visitor to Naples should leave without seeing it.

Family chapel The Sangro di Sansevero family lived next door to this chapel, and several of them are buried here. It was founded in 1590, and was completely reconstructed by Prince Raimondo di Sangro (a leading figure of the Neapolitan Enlightenment) in the 18th century. He hired the most imaginative and up-and-coming artists of the day to work on the chapel, and they produced some highly original work.

Living statues The focal point is Giuseppe Sanmartino's remarkable statue *The Veiled Christ*, from 1753. It is made from a single piece of marble, and the shrouds are so thin and lifelike that it seems almost real. A close look at His nose reveals that He is drawing His last breath. *Modesty* by Antonio Corradini also demonstrates skilful work, but is not particularly modest. *Disillusion* by Francesco Quierolo shows a figure imprisoned by a net of ignorance. The joyous ceiling fresco, *The Glories of Paradise*, was commissioned from Francesco Russo in 1749, while Prince Raimondo designed the marble floor himself. Above the entrance is a monument showing one of the Sangro family leaping out of his coffin—an inspection of the family coat of arms shows that the lion has one eye open and one shut.

Human experiments Down in the crypt are some bizarre skeletons, which show a detailed set of blood vessels. These were supposedly the results of experiments by Prince Raimondo who was a scientist, inventor and freemason, but whom many thought was also an alchemist.

HIGHLIGHTS

- *Veiled Christ*
- *Modesty* and *Disillusion*
- Grisly bodies in the crypt
- Ceiling painting, *Glories of Paradise*

INFORMATION

- 🔢 E2
- ✉ Via Francesco de Sanctis 19
- ☎ 081 551 8470
- 🕐 Wed–Mon 10–6; closed Tue
- 🍴 Cafés and restaurants in Centro Storico
- 🚇 Dante
- 🚌 201, C57, E1, R1, R4
- ♿ None
- 💷 Moderate
- 🔁 San Domenico Maggiore (➤ 44), San Lorenzo Maggiore (➤ 47), Piazza Bellini (➤ 39)

San Gregorio Armeno

INFORMATION

- ✚ E2
- ✉ Via San Gregorio Armeno 1
- ☎ 081 552 0186
- 🕐 Daily 9–12
- 🍴 Cafés and restaurants in Centro Storico
- Ⓜ Dante
- 🚌 201, C57, E1, R1, R4
- ♿ None
- 🎟 Free
- ↔ San Lorenzo Maggiore (➤ 47), Duomo (➤ 48), San Paolo Maggiore (➤ 54)
- ❓ Access to the cloisters is in Vico Giuseppe Maffei

This richly decorated and popular church has a fascinating history, some beautiful works of art, tranquil cloisters, two organs, and above all, a patron saint who works miracles.

Santa Patrizia A group of nuns settled here in the eighth century, bringing with them from Constantinople the remains of San Gregorio and Santa Patrizia. The latter has proved much more popular, and the church is sometimes known by her name. The reason for her popularity is that her blood liquefies every Tuesday (the church stays open a bit longer that day) and the miracle is said to benefit those who want children.

Wealthy convent Rebuilt in the 1500s, the convent here was particularly wealthy, with valuable paintings and other works of art. One writer said it was 'paradise on earth'. The interior is very ornate, with paintings by Neapolitan artists including Luca Giordano who portrays, above the entrance, the scene when the nuns arrived in the city. The figure showing them the way is probably a self-portrait. The ceiling is a superb 16th-century creation in carved wood, filled with detail and extending the length of the church.

Hidden cloisters Outside the church, spanning Via San Gregorio Armeno is the attractive bell tower, while around the corner is the entrance to the cloisters. Ring the bell and make your way up a grand staircase to the convent, which leads to the cloisters. These are beautifully preserved, and have a good view of the sea. In the middle of the orange and lemon trees is an enormous fountain, with life-sized statues representing the meeting of Christ and the woman at the well. It is a peaceful place, and one that is regularly used by the nuns.

San Lorenzo Maggiore

A welcome contrast to some of the city's baroque confectionery, this is an impressive Gothic church with some interesting monuments. Underneath lie the remains of a previous city.

Literary associations Two famous writers are associated with this church. Boccaccio fell in love here in 1334, and the girl he loved appears as Fiametta in his *Decameron* and other works. The poet Petrarch lived in the monastery in 1343. The monastery refectory later served as the meeting place of the parliament during the latter part of the 15th century.

Gothic purity The church was built for the Franciscan Order by Charles I and dates back to the 13th century, although there was previously a sixth-century church on the site. It acquired lavish baroque decoration through the years, which was stripped away during the 20th century to reveal the pure Gothic lines underneath. The 18th-century façade remains, and incorporates the original 14th-century wooden doors. Inside, the church is quite stark with Gothic pointed arches and single nave. The most important monument in the church is the tomb of Catherine of Austria (in the apse), beautifully sculpted by Tino di Camaino. A close look at the altar reveals 16th-century scenes of Naples.

Graeco-Roman excavations Underneath the church lies a fascinating excavation site. Extensive remains of the Roman and Greek city have been dug up, and it is possible to see the market area and, below it, a whole street of workshops, laundries and the public treasury. This is one of the most complete excavations in the Naples area and shows the way the city has occupied different levels in different ages.

HIGHLIGHTS

- Tomb of Catherine of Austria
- Altarpiece with scenes of Naples
- Original wooden entrance doors
- Graeco-Roman excavations

INFORMATION

- ✚ E2
- ✉ Via dei Tribunali 316
- ☎ 081 290 580
- 🕐 Church: daily 8–12, 5–7; excavations: Wed–Mon 9–1, 3.30–5.30; closed Tue
- 🍴 Cafés and restaurants in Centro Storico
- Ⓜ Dante
- 🚌 201, C57, E1, R1, R4
- ♿ None
- 💰 Church free, excavations inexpensive
- ↔ San Paolo Maggiore (➤ 54), Duomo (➤ 48), Pinacoteca di Girolamini (➤ 53)

Duomo

INFORMATION

Behind its austere façade is a sumptuous cathedral with many treasures. San Gennaro exerts a magnetic appeal with the mystery of his liquefying blood.

Early origins A Greek temple to Apollo probably stood on this site originally, and a church was built over it in the fourth century. That church still exists, and has been incorporated into the Duomo as the Cappella di Santa Restituta, but has been considerably modified over the centuries. Most of the original Duomo was built in the 13th century, but it has suffered several devastations through earthquakes. What you see today dates mostly from the 17th century.

Mosaics and miracles Some original columns are still in place, and some ancient frescoes can be seen. The ceiling is spectacular, with beautiful gold coffering, and there are gorgeous treasures everywhere. The baptistery is extremely old, dating from the sixth century, and has some beautiful, and very important, early mosaics. Pride of place goes to the Cappella del Tesoro di San Gennaro, with its stunning gilded dome depicting Paradise. The saint, whose body was moved here from the Catacombe San Gennaro (► 29), is credited with saving the city from disasters through the liquefaction of his blood on the first Sunday in May (the saint's feast day), and on 19 September, when the Duomo is always packed. Above the right-hand altar in the chapel there is a charming painting of the saint escaping from a furnace, by Giuseppe Ribera.

Graeco-Roman remains Beneath the Cappella di Santa Restituta lie some fascinating excavations, including Greek and Roman walls, columns and roads, a rainwater canal and some early Christian mosaics.

Pio Monte della Misericordia

Tucked away in a small church, hidden off the main street, is a staggering painting by one of the great masters, Caravaggio, which still has force today.

Good works At the beginning of the 17th century, a group of seven noblemen founded a charitable institution to help the poor and sick and also to free the Christian slaves in the Ottoman Empire. Some years later (1658–1670), a church was erected by them for the furtherance of their work. It is octagonal in shape with a loggia of five arches where the poor could shelter. The plan of the church reflects the different types of charitable activity carried out.

Caravaggio's masterpiece The main reason for any visit here is to see the superb work by Caravaggio. It hangs over the altar and is entitled *The Seven Acts of Mercy*. It has a vitality and energy that was remarkable in its time, and is still powerful today. It shows the Virgin being brought down into the city (probably representing Spaccanapoli) by two angels. The picture embraces in one scene all seven acts of mercy undertaken by the noblemen. There is a naked beggar being clothed, a tired pilgrim, a girl feeding an old prisoner with her breast milk, a corpse being wrapped by a gravedigger, and other scenes of Neapolitan life. The whole composition celebrates the love of one man for another and brings it right down to earth. The other pictures in the building pale by comparison. Each is devoted to one of the seven acts of charity. Most lively is *Liberating St. Peter from Prison* by Battistello Caracciolo, who was a pupil of Caravaggio.

Above: Caravaggio's masterpiece The Seven Acts of Mercy
Below: View of the gallery's wooden pietà

49

Pompei

INFORMATION

- ✚ F3
- ✉ Pompei Scavi, Porta Marina
- ☎ 081 857 5347
- ⏰ Daily 8.30–7.30, Apr–Oct; 8.30–5, Nov–Mar
- 🍴 Cafeteria (€€) on site, restaurants (€€–€€€) nearby
- 🚌 SITA bus from Via Pisanelli
- 🚃 Circumvesuviana: Pompei Scavi–Villa dei Misteri
- ♿ None
- 💷 Expensive
- ❓ Audio guides available

The most famous archaeological site in the world sits on Naples' doorstep, presenting an unmissable opportunity to understand more about Roman civilization and the tragedy that afflicted it.

Finds from Pompei Although the story of Pompei is very well known, a visit here is still an eye-opener. The preservation of details of the way people lived, the nitty-gritty of commercial life, the brilliance of the wall paintings, and the horrible way the city perished all make it seem that the disaster happened only yesterday. Archaeologists have worked endlessly to piece together all these elements and we are all beneficiaries of the resulting displays both here and at the Museo Archeologico Nazionale (▶ 38).

Roman city The first settlements at Pompei were probably made by farmers in the seventh century BC, but it did not become a Roman town until 80BC. For almost 160 years, it survived as an increasingly sophisticated civilization until the fatal eruption of Vesuvius in AD79. More people probably died from the toxic fumes than from volcanic ash, but that ash helped to lock the city in a time capsule. Most moving of any of the finds are the bodies of the citizens still in the same positions they were in when disaster struck.

Pompei today The entrance gate at Porta Marina is close to the forum and the basilica, bringing you straight to the commercial and political heart of the city. At the opposite end are the Teatro Grande and the Teatro Piccolo, where the citizens relaxed watching gladiatorial combats. In between are the areas where daily life was carried on, the shops, baths, inns, brothels and private houses, both of the wealthy and the working classes.

NAPLES'
best

51

Museums & Galleries

SCIENCE CITY

As part of the regeneration of the industrial areas west of the city, a new science museum (Città della Scienza) has been created. It is very well laid out and has explanations in English as well as Italian. There are plenty of hands-on exhibits to amuse all children, and it deals with current environmental issues, the origin of life and the universe. It also has a planetarium, a shop and a café.
www.cittadellascienza.it
✉ Via Coroglio 104 ☎ 081 735 2202 🕒 Tue–Sat 9–5, Sun 10–7; closed Mon and Aug 🚇 Cavalleggeri D'Aosta 🚌 C9, C10 💰 Moderate

CENTRO MUSEI DELLE SCIENZE NATURALI

The museums of anthropology, mineralogy and zoology are tucked away in the university site, but are well worth seeking out, especially the mineralogy museum. The hall itself is a superb room, and there are specimens from all over the world. Guided tours (in Italian) are available on request. (The palaeontology museum is in Largo San Marcellino 10.)
✉ Via Mezzocannone 8 ☎ 081 253 5163 🕒 Daily 9–1, Mon and Wed 3–5 🚌 24, E1, R2 💰 Inexpensive

MUSEO ARCHEOLOGICO DEI CAMPI FLEGREI

A train ride out of town, but this is a good place to go to understand the history of an area colonized by the Romans. Statues of various Roman emperors along with many other sculptures demonstrate the civilization of the time. There is also an impressive reconstruction of a *nymphaeum* (a grotto consecrated to nymphs of spring water) used in the time of Emperor Claudius, and excavated from under the water in the bay.
✉ Castello di Baia, Via Castello 39, Bacoli ☎ 081 523 3310 🕒 Daily 9–8; closed 1 Jan, 1 May, 25 Dec 🚇 Pozzuoli 🚉 Fusaro 💰 Moderate

MUSEO ARTISTICO INDUSTRIALE

Beautiful items of porcelain are held in this museum, some of them dating back to the 16th century. The museum was founded in 1878 to give young artists examples of fine workmanship, and among the pieces on show is a remarkable piece of flooring from the church of Santa Caterina a Formiello. The front portico has some remnants of the fine tiling that must once have adorned the whole frontage.
✉ Piazzetta Demetrio Salazar 6 ☎ 081 764 7471 🕒 Mon–Sat 9–1.30 🚌 C25, E5, R3 💰 Inexpensive

MUSEO DELLE CARROZZE

This small museum is located in a pavilion at the end of the garden of Villa Pignatelli. It has a collection of 19th-century Italian and French carriages.
✉ Riviera di Chiaia 200 ☎ 081 761 2356 🕒 Tue–Fri 8.30–2, Sat, Sun; hols 9–2; closed Mon 🚌 C9, C10, C24, C25, R3 💰 Inexpensive

MUSEO VILLA PIGNATELLI

Originally built for the influential aristocratic British Acton family, this fine neoclassical villa, set among

beautiful gardens, is home to the splendid Banco di Napoli collection of art. The main rooms are sumptuously decorated with richly hued furnishings and valuable antique furniture. The basement houses temporary exhibitions. It owes its name to Don Diego Aragona Pignatelli, Duke of Monteleone, who acquired it in 1867, and completely renovated it.
✉ Riviera di Chiaia 200 ☎ 081 761 2356 🕔 Tue–Fri 8.30–2, Sat, Sun; hols 9–2; closed Mon 🚌 C9, C10, C24, C25, R3 💷 Inexpensive

OSSERVATORIO ASTRONOMICO

This fine observatory, on Moiariello hill, has a wonderful position overlooking the Bay of Naples. There is an interesting museum of historic instruments, as well as a planetarium and a large lecture hall. This is a scientific institution, but it opens occasionally for special events.
www.na.astro.it ✉ Salita Moiariello 16 ☎ 081 557 5111 🕔 Guided tours only by appointment 🚌 24, R4 💷 Free

The Osservatorio Astronomico has a superb vantage point, with spectacular views over the Bay of Naples

PINACOTECA GIROLAMINI

A delightful courtyard welcomes you to this little haven of peace, where there are some outstanding examples of Renaissance art in the first floor gallery. There are good examples of Neapolitan artists, including de Ribera, Stanzione and de Simone. Look out for Dürer's painting of Girolamini, who planned this complex.
✉ Via Duomo 142 ☎ 081 449 139 🕔 Mon–Sat 9.30–1 🚌 E1, R2 💷 Free

STAZIONE ZOOLOGICA (ACQUARIO)

This institution, which also carries out scientific marine research, was founded in 1872 and is said to be one of the oldest aquariums in Europe. Examples of the sea creatures of the Bay of Naples live in seawater tanks here. (It is undergoing restoration until summer 2005.)
✉ Villa Comunale 1 ☎ 081 583 3111 🕔 Tue–Sat 9–6, Sun 9.30–7; closed Mon 🚌 C9, C10, C24, C25, R3 💷 Inexpensive

53

Churches

MAGGIO DEI MONUMENTI

Every May, Naples throws open the doors of many churches and other buildings that are normally closed so that visitors and students can find out more about the hidden side of the city (Maggio dei Monumenti; www. cib.na.cnr.it/Napoli/indice.html). In addition, artists' studios and workshops are opened to the public to reveal more of their way of life. Walks are published around different areas of the city to bring to life its historical and architectural heritage.

There is some wonderful Renaissance architecture and high-quality sculpture to be found in San Giovanni a Carbonara

SAN GIACOMO DEGLI SPAGNOLI

Hidden to the right of the town hall, this is a fascinating small church, reflecting the Spanish occupation of the city. Built in 1540, it contains the 16th-century tombs of Spanish nobles. Behind the altar is the elaborate marble tomb of Don Pedro de Toledo, who built the church.

✉ Piazza Municipio ☎ 081 552 3759 🕔 Tue–Sat 7.30–11, Sun 11–2; closed Mon 🚌 C22, C25, E5, R2, R3

SAN GIOVANNI A CARBONARA

High above its more modern brother (a church with the same name), this 14th-century chapel is one of the most historically important in the city. A steep flight of steps leads to the church intended to house the tombs of the Angevin rulers in the 15th century. There are some magnificent monuments, especially the one to King Ladislas, towering behind the altar beneath which lies the doorway to a lovely round chapel.

✉ Via San Giovanni a Carbonara 5 ☎ 081 295 873 🕔 Mon–Sat 9.30–1 🚇 Piazza Cavour, Museo 🚌 181, C68, C83

SAN PAOLO MAGGIORE

A Roman temple once stood on this site, and the pillars to Castor and Pollux from the temple can still be seen on the church façade. The double staircase leading to the entrance is most impressive. The interior is huge and has been restored since World War II. There are some lovely frescoes in the sacristy, as well as paintings by Stazione and Solimena.

✉ Piazza San Gaetano ☎ 081 454 048 🕔 Mon–Sat 9–12 🚌 E1, R2

SANT'ANGELO A NILO

Originally dating from the late 14th century, this church was substantially redesigned in the 16th century. It is notable not just for its elegant interior, but for the presence of the earliest Renaissance work in the city. This is a monument by Donatello to Cardinal Brancaccio, who built the original church—it has an interesting trompe-l'oeil effect on the front.

✉ Piazzetta Nilo ☎ 081 551 6227 🕔 Mon–Fri 10–12, 2–4 🚇 Dante 🚌 E1, R4

SANT'ANNA DEI LOMBARDI

The church is in the process of being restored, but it is worth visiting to see the fine 16th-century frescoes on the sacristy ceiling. There are many other important works in the church, including a group of terracotta statues by Mazzoni.

✉ Piazza Monteoliveto 3 ☎ 081 551 3333 ⏰ Tue–Sat 9.30–12.30 🚇 Montesanto, Funicolare Montesanto, Funicolare Augusteo 🚌 201, C57

SANTA MARIA DEGLI ANGELI

Facing a lovely piazza in the Pizzofalcone area, this church was built in the 17th century for the Princess of Sulmona. It is beautifully proportioned inside, and has some good frescoes on the vaults and the dome. There are also a number of fine paintings by Neapolitan artists.

✉ Piazza Santa Maria degli Angeli ☎ 081 764 4974 ⏰ Mon–Sat 7.30–11.30, 5–7, Sun 8.30–1.30, 6–7.30 🚌 C22, E5

SANTA MARIA DEL CARMINE

Its 75-m (246-ft) campanile is the tallest in the city, and ensures the church cannot be missed. It is a popular church, partly because of the fireworks on 16 July, which celebrate the church's feast day, but also because it has been associated with the start of the 1647 Neapolitan revolution. Inside, behind the altar, there is a much revered image of the *Madonna Bruna* (*Brown Madonna*).

✉ Piazza del Carmine ☎ 081 200 605 ⏰ Daily 6.30–12.30, 5–7.30 🚇 Piazza Garibaldi 🚌 C82, R2

SANTA MARIA DEL PARTO

Standing at the head of a steep flight of steps (or use the lift/elevator at 9B Via Francesco Caracciolo), this tiny, but atmospheric church was a beacon for sailors and has wonderful views. Built by the poet Sannazaro, who is buried here, the church has an interesting picture of *St. Michael Vanquishing the Devil* by Leonardo da Pistoia.

✉ Via Mergellina 21 ☎ 081 664 627 ⏰ Mon–Sat 5.30–8, Sun 9.30–1, 6–8 🚇 Mergellina 🚌 C16, C24, R3

SANTA MARIA DI PIEDIGROTTA

The focal point of local celebrations on 8 September, Mary's feast day, this church dates back to the 14th century. It has been much restored and now has a 19th-century façade. Among its treasures is a lovely 14th-century wooden sculpture of the *Madonna and Child* (from the Siena School), which is brought out for the celebrations.

✉ Piazza Piedigrotta 24 ☎ 081 669 761 ⏰ Mon–Sat 7–12, 5–8, Sun 7–2, 5–8 🚇 Mergellina 🚌 C16, C24, R3

CITY SPIRES

In a number of areas of the city, particularly Centro Storico, there are some remarkable spires (*guglie*), which are full of interesting detail. Guglia dell'Immacolata, in Piazza del Gesù Nuovo, is a marvellous piece of 18th-century sculpture, built for the Jesuits to celebrate important points in their teaching. Guglia di San Domenico, in Piazza San Domenico Maggiore, was begun in 1658 (but not finished until 1737) to give thanks for the end of a plague. Guglia di San Gennaro, in Piazza Riario Sforza, commemorates the saving of the city by San Gennaro from the eruption of Mount Vesuvius in 1631.

Cardinal Brancaccio's tomb, Sant'Angelo a Nilo

Parks, Gardens & Watersides

In the Top 25
◘ THE LUNGOMARE (► 31)

POSILLIPO PARKLAND

At the far end of the Posillipo promontory is a fine park with terrific views. Known variously as Parco Virgiliano or Parco della Rimembranza, it looks over the Bay of Pozzuoli and the Campi Flegrei, down to the modern developments around Coroglio and to the island of Nisida, occupied by the military. It is a wonderful place in which to enjoy the sunset.

CAPO POSILLIPO

The headland provides superb views across the Bay of Naples, and round to the Bay of Pozzuoli. Wealthy homes dot the landscape—the one closest to the edge is the Naples residence of the Italian President.
✉ Via Ferdinando Russo 🚌 140, C21

ORTO BOTANICO

One of the leading botanical gardens in Italy, this is a fascinating place to explore. The paths and lawns are full of interesting specimens, and there is a little museum in the castle in the middle (► 62).
✉ Via Foria 223 ☎ 081 449 759 🕐 Mon–Fri 9–2 🚇 Piazza Cavour, Museo 🚌 4, 15, 47, 201, CS 🎫 Free

PARCO DELLA FLORIDIANA

A spacious formal park surrounding the elegant villa (La Floridiana), this is a popular place for families and joggers. There is a big network of paths and lawns, making it a very relaxing place to wander.
✉ Via Cimarosa 77 ☎ 081 579 1776 🕐 Daily 8.30–1 hour before dusk 🚇 Vanvitelli, Funicolare Piazza Fuga 🚌 C24, C27 🎫 Free

PARCO DI CAPODIMONTE

This huge expanse (originally designed as hunting grounds for Charles III) offers plenty of opportunity to get away from the crowds surrounding the palace (► 37). There are lovely views over the city from here.
✉ Via Capodimonte ☎ 081 749 9111 🕐 8am–1 hour before dusk 🚌 24, R4 🎫 Free

PARCO VIRGILIANO

A steep climb up past the railway line brings you to a peaceful spot. Legend has it that Virgil is buried here, but in fact the monument is nothing to do with him. The poet Giacomo Leopardi is buried here, though.
✉ Salita della Grotta 20 ☎ 081 669 390 🕐 Daily 9–5 🚇 Mergellina 🚌 C16, C24, R3 🎫 Free

PORTICCIOLO DI MERGELLINA

Small fishing boats jostle with more expensive yachts in the marina. Brightly hued huts house fishermen's tackle, and popular ice-cream chalets face the sea.
✉ Via Francesco Caracciolo 🚇 Mergellina 🚌 C16, C24, R3

VILLA COMUNALE

This waterfront park has room for families, visitors and joggers. It was created in the 18th century, and has wide avenues, winding paths, statues, fountains and a splendid bandstand, built in 1887.
✉ Riviera di Chiaia 🚌 C9, C10, C24, C25

The so-called 'Tomb of Virgil' high up in the peaceful Parco Virgiliano

Markets

FIERA ANTIQUARIA NAPOLETANA
This vibrant market along the seafront has antiques, silver, paintings and much more. Not everything is genuine, but bargains will almost certainly be found.
✉ Villa Comunale 🕐 From 7am last Sun of month 🚌 C9, C10, C24, C25, R3

MERCATINO DELLA PIGNASECCA
Food and delicacies, household items and clothes can all be found at this bustling market which runs all the way down Via Pignasecca from Piazzetta Montesanto.
✉ Piazzetto Montesanto 🕐 Daily 8–1 Ⓜ Montesanto, Funicolare Montesanto 🚌 C57, E2

MERCATINO DELLA TORRETTA
This is one of the few covered markets in the city, and sells local foodstuffs. There is also a good choice of clothes, some of them of very good quality.
✉ Viale Antonio Gramsci 🕐 Daily 9–1 Ⓜ Mergellina 🚌 C16, C24, R3

MERCATINO DI ANTIGNANO
This civilized market, which runs through the streets between Via Mario Fiore and Piazza degli Artisti, has good bargains in smart clothes and shoes as well as food and bootleg CDs.
✉ Piazza degli Artisti 🕐 Mon–Sat 8–1 Ⓜ Vanvitelli, Funicolare Piazza Fuga 🚌 C24, C27, E4, R1

MERCATO DEI FIORI
This market is only for the early riser and is usually over by around 8am. Held along the moat of Castel Nuovo, it is principally for the city's street vendors.
✉ Via Ferdinando Acton 🕐 Daily at dawn 🚌 C25

MERCATO DEL CASALE DI POSILLIPO
Clothes and shoes are the main items sold in this pleasant market held along the tree-lined Viale Virgilio in Posillipo.
✉ Viale Virgilio 🕐 Thu 8–2 🚌 140, C27, C31

MERCATO DI SANT'ANTONIO ABATE
This is a popular food market with the locals. Browse down this long street and end up at Porta Capuana (Mon–Sat), where there are clothes and shoes.
✉ Via Sant'Antonio Abate 🕐 Daily 9–8 🚌 14, 147, 182, 201, C68, R5

MERCATO PORTA NOLANA
This evocative market is the best place in the city to buy fish, but there are also other foods. It merges with the market in Piazza Garibaldi and nearby streets, where there are all kinds of electronic items.
✉ Via Nolana 🕐 8–2 🚌 R2

THE PICK OF PIGNASECCA

The market at Pignasecca runs in front of a number of shops that have particularly interesting food for sale. Look out for:

Antica Panettaria (✉ Via Pignasecca 20), where dozens of different breads can be found.

Fiorenzano (✉ Via Pignasecca 48/50) for something to eat, either a quick slice of pizza or some *tavola calda*.

Pescheria Azzurra (✉ Via Portamedina 4), with its wonderful displays of fish against bright blue tiles.

Salumeria Rognoni (✉ Via Pignasecca 38) stacked high with different meats and cheeses.

Vibrant pavement stalls filled with fresh produce at the Mercato Porta Nolana

Streets & Piazzas

PALAZZI IN VIA TOLEDO

Look above the shop fronts in Via Toledo and you will see the façades of many historic *palazzi*. The oldest, dating from the 16th century are:
Palazzo Tocco di Montemileto (No. 148)
Palazzo Buono (No. 340; now Rinascenta department store)
Palazzo della Nunziator a Apostolica (No. 352).

Particularly significant are:
Palazzo Berio (No. 265), which was designed by Luigi Vanvitelli in the 18th century
Palazzo di Domenico Barbaja (No. 205), where composer Gioacchino Rossini lived from 1815 to 1822
Palazzo Zevallos Colonna di Stigliano (No. 188), whose entrance was designed by Cosimo Fanzago, the city's major architect in the 17th century.

Other *palazzi* to note are:
Palazzo Monaco di Lapio (No. 308)
Palazzo Lieto (No. 317)
Palazzo Cavalcanti (No. 349)
Palazzo della Porta (No. 369).

CORSO UMBERTO I

Naples was devastated by cholera in 1884 and, as a consequence, a major urban renewal project was undertaken, which lasted until the early part of the 20th century. One of the results was this impressive road, also known as *Il Rettifilo* (literally 'straight line'). The university and a motley assortment of shops, ranging from the speciality pen shop to cut-price clothes markets, have their homes along here.
🚌 148, C55, E1, R2

PEDAMENTINA

A steep flight of steps, not all of which are in good condition, leads down the hill from Castel Sant'Elmo to Corso Vittorio Emanuele, and it's a good idea to take this path going down rather than up. The views of the bay and over the city are magnificent, but the immediate environment is often made up of dilapidated houses and poor living conditions. It is, however, a most scenic walk.
🚇 Vanvitelli, Funicolare Piazza Fuga 🚌 C28, C31

PIAZZA DANTE

A statue of Dante lords it over this large piazza, which has been restored to become quite elegant. It was originally called Largo del Mercatello and was a market just outside the city walls. Redesigned by Vanvitelli in the 18th century to house the palace of King Charles III, it retains its stately aura. On one side is Port'Alba, a good hunting ground for second-hand books.
🚇 Dante 🚌 201, C57, E1, R1, R4

PIAZZA GIOVANNI BOVIO

Currently disrupted by ongoing building work on the Metro (subway), this piazza was part of the 19th-century urban renewal scheme that created Corso Umberto I. The Stock Exchange used to sit on one side of it, but the building is now used by the Chamber of Commerce.
🚌 148, C55, CS, E1, R1, R2, R3

QUARTIERI SPAGNOLI

Spanish troops originally occupied these crowded tenements to the west of Via Toledo, but now they are home to the poorest people in the city. The streets are narrow and festooned with washing; children shout and play in the street, and motorcycles

scream up and down. Yet, there are interesting churches and characteristic restaurants hidden away, and it is enjoyable to stroll here in daylight (but not after dark).
🚇 Funicolare Toledo 🚌 201, C25, C27, E3, E5, R3

VIA ANTICAGLIA

Three Roman roads originally ran through the city: Via dei Tribunali, Spaccanapoli (➤ 43), and this one. Now the quietest of them all, the Via Anticaglia is an interesting road to explore for the remains of earlier times. Arches across the street used to link the bathhouse with the playhouse, where Emperor Nero once performed. Via Sapienza, Via Pisanelli and Via Santi Apostoli also made up the original Roman road.
🚇 Museo, Piazza Cavour 🚌 201, C57, E1, R1, R4

VIA CHIAIA

Smart clothes shops line the sides of this elegant street, which was constructed in the 16th century.
About halfway down, it is crossed by a huge arch, which carries Via Giovanni Nocotera over to Pizzofalcone. Lifts (elevators) and stairs can take you up there. The name means 'beach' and the road once went directly to the coast.
🚌 C9, C10, C22, C24, C25, E3, R3

Flags take the place of washing during an Easter festival in the narrow streets of the Quartieri Spagnoli

VIA SCARLATTI

Vomero hill is one of the smarter parts of town, and this street is the smartest in Vomero. It is pedestrianized and lined with plane trees and classy shops. The most elegant buildings were constructed in the 19th century, but there are some less attractive recent additions. A happy afternoon could be spent shopping here, with breaks for cakes and ice creams.
🚇 Vanvitelli, Funicolare Piazza Fuga, Funicolare Via Morghen 🚌 C24, C27, E4

VIA TOLEDO

Mostly pedestrianized, this is a smart shopping street, marking the eastern edge of the Quartieri Spagnoli. It is lined with historic *palazzi* and interspersed with shops and churches. Until recently it was called Via Roma, and is sometimes called that today. It was originally built in the 16th century and used to be one of Europe's most elegant streets.
🚇 Funicolare Augusteo 🚌 C25, C57, E3, E5, R3

59

Best of Pompei

In the Top 25
25 POMPEI (▶ 50)

FORUM

This is the oldest part of Pompei and is built at the highest point. The forum was central to political and commercial life, and faces the basilica (law courts) and the Temple of Apollo on one side, and the temples of Jupiter and Vespasian on the other sides. The forum dates from at least the second century BC.
✉ Via del Foro

HOUSE OF JULIA FELIX

This large property belonged to a very wealthy Pompei resident. Not all of it was used as the owner's accommodation—some was let out to rent, as homes and shops. It also contained baths that were open to the public, and a large waiting area in the courtyard.
✉ Via dell'Abbondanza

HOUSE OF THE CITARISTA

Two houses originally existed here, and there are several courtyards. The house takes its name from a statue of Apollo playing a lyre, which is now housed in the Museo Archeologico Nazionale (▶ 38).
✉ Via Stabiana

HOUSE OF THE FAUN

One of the most important and famous private houses in the city, it is also one of the largest. The wealth of the original owners is displayed in the beautiful wall paintings and in the tiled mosaics. A copy of the captivating statue that gives the house its name stands in the middle of the *impluvium* (pond).
✉ Via Della Fortuna

HOUSE OF THE GOLDEN CUPIDS

Head for the bedroom of this house to see the lovely gold cupids that decorate it and after which it is named. It is not a particularly large house, but it has some attractive wall paintings and a well-restored garden, with a pool and sculptures, that recaptures what life must have been like for the wealthy Pompeians.
✉ Vicolo dei Vetti

HOUSE OF THE MYSTERIES

The best-preserved frescoes in Pompei can be found here. Bright and vibrant, they tell the story of a young bride apparently being initiated into the cult of Dionysus, which was popular here in the second century BC. The architecture of the house is interesting. It was originally an urban villa, but was

DON'T MISS

Pompei is so full of interesting ruins that it is difficult to take them all in. The main attractions are listed on this page, but other places worth seeing are:
Herculaneum Gate (✉ Via dei Sepolcri), which leads to Naples and Herculaneum. It is a beautiful gate with three archways, two for pedestrians and the central one for carriages.
House of Menander (✉ Via dell'Abbondanza), named after a Greek comic poet, whose portrait is among the many fine paintings here.
House of the Tragic Poet (✉ Via di Terme), a middle-class house with a mosaic saying 'beware of the dog'.
House of Venus (✉ Via dell'Abbondanza), with its lovely fresco of Venus riding in a shell.
Macellum (✉ Via degli Augustali) was the covered meat and fish market, part of the busy shopping area around the forum.

converted into a country residence around 60BC. It would once have had an excellent view of the sea.
✉ Via dei Sepolcri

HOUSE OF THE VETII

This house was owned by wealthy merchants, and it has a great many well-preserved murals. They show cupids and many characters from Greek mythology. Its main attraction, however, is the small room near the kitchen that features famous erotic paintings. Don't forget to look at the lovely garden.
✉ Vicolo dei Vetii

THEATRES

The large theatre, holding about 5,000 people, was built in the second century BC. It had a wonderful setting, with the Lattari mountains in the background, and it also had a large awning to protect the spectators from the strong sun. There is a smaller theatre (or Odeon) nearby that was intended for musical performances and political assemblies. Behind the buildings were the barracks for the gladiators who performed in the amphitheatre to the east of the city.
✉ Via Nocera

The amphitheatre at Pompei, one of the oldest of its kind in existence, had once seen more stirring action

VIA DEI SEPOLCRI

The surface of this solemn road is still indented with the wheel tracks of the carriages that used to enter the city. Lying outside the city walls, it is lined with the tombs of the main families of the city. It was a popular Roman custom to do this, and it was considered a sign of respect to be buried here. Several tombs carry inscriptions with information about the family concerned.

VIA DELL'ABBONDANZA

Walking down this street you can imagine the daily life of the city. It is lined with shops, such as the bakery and tannery, with inns where you can see pictures of the waitresses, and with private houses entered by narrow entrance doorways. The road also leads to the public baths and to the brothel.

61

Free Places

┌─ In the Top 25
│ **⑤ CASTEL DELL'OVO (► 30)**
└─

MORE FOR FREE

Places to visit free of charge are also listed in other sections of this book. They are:
Orto Botanico (► 56)
Osservatorio Astronomico (► 53; by appointment)
Pinacoteca Girolamini (► 53).
In addition, all parks and gardens are free, as is entrance to many (but not all) of the churches.

L'ARCHIVIO FOTOGRAFICO PARISIO

Parisio was a photographer who recorded most aspects of 20th-century daily life in Naples and Campania. Over 100,000 photographs recall how the city and its people looked before the destruction in World War II, providing a fascinating view of events during and after that period. He was also a very innovative and experimental photographer.

✉ Piazza del Plebiscito ☎ 081 764 5122 ⏰ Daily 9.30–1.30 🚡 Funicolare Augusteo 🚌 201, C25, C57, E3, E5, R3 💷 Free

CRYPTA NEAPOLITANA

A road tunnel was constructed in the first century BC, linking Naples to Pozzuoli, which was in use until the middle of the 19th century. There have been a number of landslides, and the tunnel is now blocked, although you can climb above it and look down at the parts which survive today. It is worth visiting both because of its antiquity, and to see the remains.

✉ Via della Grotta Vecchia ⏰ Daily 9–1 🚇 Piazza Leopardi 🚌 C9, C10 💷 Free

NAPOLI NELLA RACCOLTA DE MURA

Hidden down a flight of steps opposite Café le Professore, this is a wonderfully evocative collection of posters and photographs recalling the heyday of Neapolitan song and some Neapolitan characters. There is usually background music of some of the famous numbers, which helps to create the right mood.

✉ Piazza Trieste e Trento ☎ 081 420 3331 ⏰ Mon–Sat 9–6, Sun 9–1 🚡 Funicolare Augusteo 🚌 201, C25, C57, E3, E5, R3 💷 Free

ORTO BOTANICO MUSEUM

In the middle of the botanical gardens is a bright pink 17th-century castle, which houses an interesting museum. The first item to greet you looks like a piece of abstract art, but it is in fact a way of tracing the evolution of plants. Other exhibits display fossils and plants, and there is a fascinating section on the arts and crafts of Latin America and Southeast Asia.

✉ Via Foria 223 ☎ 081 449 759 ⏰ Mon–Fri 9–2 🚇 Piazza Cavour, Museo 🚌 4, 15, 47, 201, CS 💷 Free

PALAZZO DELLO SPAGNOLA

Tucked away in the Sanità area is a superbly restored *palazzo* that is not always open to the public but is well worth going to look at. It was built in 1738 for the Moscati family by architect Ferdinando Sanfelice, and it has a double flying staircase that can be seen from the courtyard.

✉ Via dei Virgine 19 🚇 Piazza Cavour 🚌 4, 15, 47, 201, CS 💷 Free

NAPLES
where to...

Elegant Dining

PRICES

Expect to pay per person for a two-course meal, excluding drink:

€ up to €15
€€ up to €50
€€€ over €50

AUGUST HOLIDAYS

It will be disappointing for those who visit at the height of summer, but many restaurants in Naples close for some, or all of August. The Feast of the Assumption (*Ferragosto*) is on 15 August and it is celebrated all over the city, but many businesses will be closed at that time.

A CANZUNCELLA (€€€)

Traditional Neapolitan music is the theme here, where the food and service are of a high standard. On Saturday evenings, you can enjoy a banquet and a concert.
✉ Piazza S Maria la Nova 18 ☎ 081 558 9018 ⏰ Eve only; closed Tue 🚌 C25, R1, R2, R3, R4

LA BERSAGLIERA (€€€)

Once frequented by celebrities, this atmospheric restaurant in the shadow of Castel dell'Ovo serves traditional Italian dishes.
✉ Borgo Marinaro 10 ☎ 081 746 6016 ⏰ Closed Tue 🚌 C25

LA CANTINELLA (€€€)

One of Naples' most famous and expensive restaurants, this has a luxurious atmosphere, and is renowned for its fine seafood dishes and splendid antipasto.
www.lacantinella.it ✉ Via Nazario Sauro 23 ☎ 081 764 8684 ⏰ Closed Sun and May–Oct 🚌 C25

CARUSO (€€€)

This elegant restaurant, named after the singer, is on the top floor of Grand Hotel Vesuvio. Superb views of the Bay of Naples complement expertly prepared dishes.
www.vesuvio.it ✉ Via Partenope 45 ☎ 081 764 0520 ⏰ Daily 🚌 C25

CIRO A SANTA BRIGIDA (€€€)

A popular restaurant with a well-deserved reputation. The owner is behind a move to enhance the quality of pizzas and has developed the 'Pizza Napoletana' logo to show where the best examples may be found.
✉ Via Santa Brigida 71 ☎ 081 552 4072 ⏰ Closed Sun 🚌 C25, R3

DA DORA (€€€)

This small restaurant serves up really memorable seafood meals, so be sure to book. House specials include tagliatelle with sea urchins, *mezzanello* (rich pasta dish with seafood) and oysters.
✉ Via F Palasciano 30 ☎ 081 68 0519 ⏰ 8pm–midnight; closed Sun 🚌 140, C9, C10, C24, C28, R3

LA SACRESTIA (€€€)

Out at Mergellina, this is one of the most highly regarded restaurants in the city. Cooking combines traditional Neapolitan dishes with more contemporary innovations.
✉ Via Orazio 116 ☎ 081 761 1051 ⏰ Closed Sun dinner and Mon lunch 🚇 Mergellina 🚌 C16, C24, R3

SIMPOSIUM (€€€)

You need to book ahead to eat here. The meals are re-creations of Neapolitan recipes from the past and are laid on as formal banquets at a communal table accompanied by music from the relevant period.
www.gastronomiastorica.it ✉ Via Benedetto Croce 38 ☎ 081 551 8510 ⏰ Fri 9pm–midnight, Sat 1–4 and 9–midnight, Sun 1–4 🚇 Dante 🚌 E1, R4

Neapolitan & Seafood Restaurants

ANTICA OSTERIA PISANO (€)

A friendly family restaurant, serving beautifully prepared local dishes (which vary according to what is in the market) and desserts.

✉ Piazzetta Crocele ai Mannesi 1–4 ☎ 081 554 8325 ⏰ Mon–Sat 12.30–3.30, 7.30–11; closed Sun 🚌 148, C55, C58, R2

BELLINI (€€)

You can enjoy large and very satisfying meals of pasta and, particularly, seafood, such as the *linguine ai frutti di mare*. Service can be slow.

✉ Via Santa Maria di Costantopoli 79/80 ☎ 081 459 774 ⏰ Mon–Sat 12.30–3.30, 7.30–11; closed Sun and Jul–Sep 🚇 Dante 🚌 C57, E1, R1, R4

LA CANTINA DEL SOLE (€€)

There is a wide-ranging menu here with some unusual and historic dishes, but let the patron explain it and then enjoy the superb local delicacies.

✉ Via G Paladino 3 ☎ 081 552 7312 ⏰ Tue–Sat 7–midnight, Sun 1–3.30, 7–midnight; closed Mon 🚇 Dante 🚌 C36, E1

LA CANTINA DI SICA (€€)

This Vomero restaurant is beloved of artists and writers and many have left a poem or sketch on the walls. A good choice of local specialities.

✉ Via Bernini Gian Lorenzo ☎ 081 556 7520 ⏰ Closed Tue and Sun eve 🚇 Vanvitelli, Fonicolare Piazza Fuga, Fonicolare Via Morghen 🚌 C24, C27

HOSTERIA TOLEDO (€€)

There is a friendly family atmosphere in this restaurant, a supporter of the 'Slow Food' (▶ 67) movement, which started in Italy, and is now worldwide. Don't be afraid to try the 'Chef's Surprise'.

www.hosteriatoledo.it ✉ Vico Giardinetto 78/A ☎ 081 421 257 ⏰ Noon–3, 7–1; closed Tue eve 🚇 Funicolare Augusteo 🚌 C25, C57, E3, E5, R3

RISTORANTE AL 53 (€)

This busy restaurant has a good position looking out over Piazza Dante, and serves a good range of well-prepared food at reasonable prices. The service is efficient, but the wine list is limited.

✉ Piazza Dante 53 ☎ 081 549 9372 ⏰ Daily 8pm–1am 🚇 Dante 🚌 C57, R1, R4

TERRAZZA CALABRITTO (€€)

A very friendly restaurant with a lively bar downstairs, where you may sometimes find complimentary antipasto to nibble. Upstairs, the smart restaurant serves superb food, especially fish, which is cooked gently and slowly.

✉ Piazza Vittoria 1 ☎ 081 240 5188 ⏰ Daily 12.30–3, 7.30–11 🚌 4, C24, E5, R3

VADINCHENIA (€€€)

A modern restaurant with contemporary decoration, it serves some very imaginative dishes at reasonable prices.

✉ Via Pontano 21 ☎ 081 661 958/081 660 117 ⏰ 8pm–1am; closed Sun 🚌 C24, C27

NEAPOLITAN COOKING

Traditional Neapolitan cooking is simple, and uses fresh ingredients. Developed by the Angevins in the 13th century and perfected by the Bourbons in the 18th century, it has a long and distinguished history. One of the most popular dishes is *spaghetti alle vongole* (with clams), and another is *parmigiana di melanzane* (aubergines/eggplant with cheese). Fish, of course, features strongly on most menus and is sometimes cooked *all'acquapazza*–a method of cooking used by local fishermen for centuries where a small amount of water is added to the ingredients, blending them together and giving a particularly fresh taste. A traditional meat dish is *braciolone napoletano* (rich, filling meat loaf).

Pizzerie & Budget Restaurants

HOME OF THE PIZZA

Naples is well known as the home of the pizza. Its history goes back to Roman, or even Greek, days when Neapolis was a Greek colony. A recipe was found in the ruins of Pompeii for a kind of pizza that was eaten in the Naples area. At that time it was just a plain dough, but in the 16th century tomatoes were introduced into Europe from Peru. They were initially thought to be poisonous, but the poor people of Naples mixed them with their dough and produced the first pizzas as we would recognize them. They were soon declared to be the best in Italy, and their popularity spread, even to royalty. They were introduced into America in the 19th century, and are now found all over the world. But the best pizzas are still found in Naples.

ACUNZO (€€)

A busy pizzeria in the Vomero district, with an excellent selection of different toppings to accompany. Also offers typical regional dishes in a wider menu.

✉ Via Cimarosa 60 ☎ 081 578 5362 🕓 11.30–midnight; closed Sun 🚇 Piazza Fuga 🚌 C28, C31, C32, V1

ANTICA PIZZERIA DELL'ANGELO (€€)

Making a delicious variation from the normal style of pizza, crusts at this pizzeria are filled with one of three cheese or ham stuffings. Try it when you are in Centro Storico.

✉ Piazzetta del Nilo 16 ☎ 081 542 2001 🕓 Daily 11–4 🚇 Dante 🚌 C36, E1

ANTONIO & ANTONIO (€€)

This restaurant has a splendid view over the waterfront and the bay. The food is equally good with classic pizzas as well as a wider and very inventive menu.

✉ Via Francesco Crispi 89 🕓 12.15–3, 7.20–midnight; closed Mon 🚇 Dante 🚌 C24, C27

BRANDI (€€)

Pizza Margherita was supposedly invented here, and its reputation has attracted the likes of Bill Clinton when he was here for the G7 summit. The pizzas are extremely good, and there is also a wider menu. The setting, in a narrow street off Via Chiaia, is most evocative.

www.brandi.it ✉ Salita Sant'Anna di Palazzo 1 ☎ 081 416 928 🕓 12.30–3.30, 7.30–midnight; closed Mon 🚌 C22, C25, R3

DA CARMINE (€)

A simple but very central restaurant, with tasty cooking which uses fresh ingredients.

✉ Via dei Tribunali 330 ☎ 081 294 383 🕓 Closed Sun, Mon and Tue eve 🚇 Dante 🚌 C36, E1

CIRO A MERGELLINA (€€)

With an attractive Mergellina waterfront setting, this popular restaurant specializes in excellent pizzas, as well as a good range of antipasto.

✉ Via Mergellina 17/21 ☎ 081 681 780 🕓 Daily 1–4, 7.30–1, Jun–Sep; closed Mon, Oct–May 🚇 Mergellina 🚌 C16, C24, R3

LOMBARDI A SANTA CHIARA (€€)

One of the most popular pizza restaurants in Centro Storico, this has a good menu and wine list, as well as excellent pizzas.

✉ Via Benedetto Croce 59 ☎ 081 552 0780 🕓 Mon–Sat noon–4, 8–midnight 🚇 Dante 🚌 C36, E1

MARINO (€€)

This well-known restaurant close to the waterfront is famous for its pizzas, which are served in a bright, fresh blue dining room.

✉ Via Santa Lucia 118/120 ☎ 081 764 0280 🕓 Noon–3.30, 7–1.30; closed Mon 🚌 C25

MASANIELLO (€€)

In the courtyard of an old *palazzo* in Centro Storico, this place serves terrific pizzas, especially those with sausage or rocket (arugula). There is also a good range of other Neapolitan dishes.

✉ Via Donalbina 28 ☎ 081 552 8863 🕐 Closed Mon and Fri 🚍 201, C57, R1

MATTOZZI (€)

A popular restaurant in a central area, this place is famous for its superb range of good value pizzas.

✉ Piazza Carità 2 ☎ 081 552 4322 🕐 Noon–3.30, 7–12.30 🚠 Funicolare Augusteo 🚍 24, 201, E2, R1

DA MICHELE (€)

A very basic restaurant, serving only two types of pizza, but the fantastic value attracts hordes of people, so be prepared to wait.

✉ Via Cesare Sersale 1/3 ☎ 081 553 9204 🕐 Mon–Sat 10am–11pm; closed Sun 🚇 Piazza Garibaldi 🚍 R2

OSTERIA CASTELLO (€)

This friendly family restaurant serves delicious home-made food, including pasta with ham and red peppers. They also have wonderful desserts, if you have any room left.

✉ Via Santa Teresa a Chiaia 38 ☎ 081 400 486 🕐 1.30–3.30, 8–midnight; closed Sun 🚇 Piazza Amedeo 🚍 C22, C25, R3

PORT'ALBA (€)

One of the oldest pizza restaurants in the city (dating from 1830).

Their food is extremely good value, particularly the delicious pizzas.

✉ Via Port'Alba 18 ☎ 081 459 713 🕐 Daily 1–3, 5–midnight 🚇 Dante 🚍 C57, R1, R4

IL RE DI NAPOLI (€)

A good place for people-watching on the seafront, this place serves interesting stuffed pizzas named after kings, as well as more conventional toppings.

✉ Via Partenope 29/30 ☎ 081 764 7775 🕐 Daily 12.30–4, 7.30–1 🚍 C25

DA TONINO (€)

This small, friendly restaurant and *enoteca*, with its delicious home-cooked food and terrific range of wines, is said to be one of the oldest trattorie in Naples.

✉ Via Santa Theresa a Chiaia 47 ☎ 081 421 533 🕐 Closed Sun 🚍 C24, C25, C26, C27, C28

TRIANON PIZZERIA (€)

There is a huge variety of pizzas at this long-established restaurant. While it can get crowded and chaotic, it is still worth visiting. Upstairs there is attractive art nouveau decoration.

✉ Via Pietro Colletta 42/46 ☎ 081 553 9426 🕐 11–3.30, 6.30–12.30 🚇 Piazza Garibaldi 🚍 R2

VINARIUM (€€)

A relaxed atmosphere and good food make this an enjoyable place to come. The excellent wine list completes the experience.

✉ Via Capella Vecchia 7 ☎ 081 764 4114 🕐 Mon–Fri 10.30am–2.30am, Sat 7pm–2.30am 🚍 4, C24, E5, R3

SLOW FOOD

Back in 1986, as a reaction to the opening of a fast-food restaurant in a beautiful Italian piazza, the 'Slow Food' movement was born. Its aims are to celebrate the qualities of individual foods, and to uphold the food traditions of different areas. 'Slow Food' advocates maintain that the uniformity of food found in supermarkets and fast-food restaurants is not inevitable, but that food can be full of taste and unique. The movement started in Italy, but has now spread to many countries worldwide.

Bars & Cafés

MORE BARS AND CAFÉS

Naples is packed with bars and cafés. Some other good places to enjoy are **Bar Brasiliano** (✉ Galleria Umberto I 78 ☎ 081 418 383), which has plenty of chairs in the Galleria; **Caffè Novecento** (✉ Calita Trinità Maggiore 4 ☎ 081 552 1433), where they serve 32 types of chocolate drink and 44 types of tea, and **Gran Caffè La Caffetiera** (✉ Piazza dei Martiri 30 ☎ 081 764 4243), an elegant café on the piazza with an excellent range of pastries.

COFFEE CHECK

Coffee to the Neapolitans is like a religion. They claim to have the best coffee in Italy, and they drink it strong and sweet. Special coffees to look out for are:
corretto – espresso with a dash of grappa
freddo – iced coffee
lungo – slightly less concentrated form of the normal very strong espresso
macchiato – espresso with a dash of milk
nocciola – espresso with a sweet hazelnut froth.

BAR NILO (€)

A small bar, popular especially for coffee and a snack (taken standing up, as Neapolitans do). They also sell aperitifs, and a range of panini and sweet pastries. Nilo (the ancient Eygptian river god, Nile) is the symbol of the city.
✉ Via San Biagio dei Librai 129/130 ☎ 081 551 7029 🕒 Daily 6.30am–9pm 🚌 148, C55, C58, E1, R2

BAR ROSATA (€€)

This popular bar is right in the heart of the tourist area, with seats overlooking the piazza. Service is efficient, and they serve a range of pizzas, snacks and drinks. Try their hazelnut and chocolate coffee.
✉ Piazza Trieste e Trento ☎ 081 421 660 🕒 Daily 7.30am–1am 🚌 C25, R3

CAFFÈ GAMBRINUS (€€)

One of the most famous cafés in the city, this is an enjoyable place in which to sit and watch the crowds, or to revel in the sophistication of the tea bar inside.
✉ Via Chiaia 1/2 ☎ 081 417 582 🕒 Daily 8am–1.30am 🚌 C25, R3

CAFFÈ MEXICO (€)

This café has one of the best reputations in the city. The coffee is roasted on the premises, and there are many blends, which are packaged up very attractively and make good gifts.
✉ Piazza Dante 86 ☎ 081 549 9330 🕒 Mon–Sat 7.30am–8.30pm 🚊 Dante 🚌 24, R1, R4

GRAN BAR RIVIERA (€€)

This stylish waterfront bar has a wide selection of pastries and drinks. It is great for people-watching at any time of the day, but gets very busy in the evening.
✉ Riviera di Chiaia 181/183 ☎ 081 665 026 🕒 Daily 8.30am–1am 🚊 Tram 1 🚌 C9, C18, C24, C25, C28, R3

GRAN CAFFÈ ARAGONESE (€€)

Relax here and watch life buzzing round the piazza. There is a wide choice of delicacies, and snacks all day long. You can also get breakfast.
www.grancaffearagonese.it
✉ Piazza San Domenica Maggiore 5/8 ☎ 081 552 8740 🕒 Daily 8.30am–1am 🚊 Dante 🚌 C36, E1

GRAN CAFFÈ DUOMO (€€)

This pretty café, near the Duomo, serves a selection of pastries and cakes and great coffee throughout the day.
✉ Via Duomo 163/165 ☎ 081 297 078 🕒 Daily 7.30am–8.30pm 🚌 148, C55, C58, E1, R2

DA MA L.U.I.S.E. (€)

This convenient café near the Centrale funicular station has a terrific range of snacks, both sweet and savoury. There are tables outside, but plenty of space inside to eat on the go. There is another, branch in Piazza Martiri.
✉ Via Toledo 266 ☎ 081 415 367 🕒 Mon–Sat 8am–8.30pm, Sun 9.30am–2.30pm 🚊 Funicolare Centrale 🚌 C25, R3

Takeaway & Tavola Calda

AUGUSTUS (€€)

At the back of this bar there are trays of marinated delights. You can either sit there and enjoy your selection, or eat it as you go along. They sell good buffalo mozzarella and their pastries are irresistible.

✉ Via Toledo 147 ☎ 081 551 3540 🕒 Daily 9am–7pm 🚇 Funicolare Augusteo 🚌 E1, E2, R1

CAFFÈ ROMA (€€)

One of the smarter places in Via Toledo, this café serves an enticing range of both savoury and sweet delicacies. Join the others standing at the bar enjoying their snack —it is cheaper that way.

✉ Via Toledo 325 ☎ 081 406 832 🕒 6am–10.30pm; closed Sat eve 🚇 Funicolare Augusteo 🚌 E1, E2, R1

E' SCUGNIZZ' (€)

The formal Galleria Umberto I has a number of cafés, but this has one of the best selections of *tavola calda*. There are chairs and tables outside for people-watching.

✉ Galleria Umberto I 72 ☎ 081 401 199 🕒 8am–midnight 🚌 C25, R3

LA FOCACCIA (€)

This place serves fresh, focaccia with toppings like peppers and potato. They also do pizza slices, and have a great selection of beers. A good place to stop after a late night in the local bars.

✉ Via Benedetto de Croce 31 ☎ 081 412 277 🕒 Mon–Sat 10am–2am, Sun 6pm–3am 🚌 C22, C25

FRIGGITORE VOMERO (€)

Specializes in fried snacks, such as zucchini (courgettes), *zeppole* (dough balls) and *graffe* (doughnuts), which are just right for a quick breakfast, or a light sightseeing meal.

✉ Via Domenico Cimarosa 44 ☎ 081 578 3130 🕒 Mon–Fri 9–2, 5–10, Sat 5–midnight; closed Sun 🚇 Vanvitelli, Funicolare Piazza Fuga 🚌 C28, C31, C32

GASTRONOMIA FIORENZANO (€)

This is a good place to stop while exploring the Pignasecca market. They serve snacks and fried delicacies, as well as full meals and wine.

✉ Via Pignasecca 48/49/50 ☎ 081 552 3663 🕒 10.30am–midnight; closed Sun 🚇 Funicolare Montesanto 🚌 24, 201, E2, R1

IMPERIAL COFFEE (€€)

The large café facing onto the piazza has a wide choice of *tavola calda* and other house specials. Select from the counters inside, then relax in the open air and watch the crowds.

✉ Piazza Carità 42/44 ☎ 081 580 2560 🚇 Funicolare Augusteo 🚌 24, 201, E2, R1

DI MATTEO (€)

The most popular takeaway (take-out) in the city, it usually has queues, but the pizzas and the fried specials are terrific.

✉ Via dei Tribunali 94 ☎ 081 294 203 🕒 Mon–Sat 10am–midnight; closed Sun 🚇 Dante 🚌 E1, R4

TAVOLA CALDA

A buffet of hot dishes is known as a *tavola calda*. It includes simple meat, egg and vegetable dishes that can be eaten alone or combined together for something more substantial. Many cafés have an area at the back devoted to this type of buffet, which often heaves with the great variety of different dishes.

Pasticcerie & Gelaterie

SFOGLIATELLE

This Naples delicacy is made from the lightest puff pastry or shortcrust pastry with a filling of ricotta and cinnamon or citrus, and made in the shape of a shell. They can be found all over the city, and most of them are very good. They were originally made in the local monasteries, but in 1818, Pasquale Pintauro started to produce them commercially and served them hot. It is still possible to buy *sfogliatelle* at the **Pintauro** bakery (✉ Via Toledo 275 ☎ 081 417 339).

BILANCIONE

Opinions vary about who makes the best ice cream in Naples, but this place must have the best view. There is a huge choice of ices to enjoy while gazing over the Bay of Naples. ✉ Via Posillipo 238/B ☎ 081 769 1923 ◷ Tue–Fri 7am–11pm, Sat and Sun 7am–1am, Nov–Feb; Tue–Sun 5pm–1am, Aug; Tue–Sun 7am–1am rest of year ▢ 140

CHALET CIRO

The Mergellina chalets used to be fashionable places to come to. Still popular, Chalet Ciro has been serving a delicious range of ices and cakes for over 50 years. www.chaletciro.it ✉ Via Caracciolo ☎ 081 669 928 ◷ Mon, Tue, Thu–Sun 7am–2am ◉ Mergellina ▢ 140, C16, C24, R3

FANTASIA GELATI

An exotic range of ice cream combinations can be had here. There are other branches at Via Toledo 381 and Via Cilea 80. ✉ Piazza Vanvitelli ☎ 081 578 8383 ◷ Daily 7am–midnight ◉ Vanvitelli, Funicolare Piazza Fuga ▢ C28, C31, C32

GELATERIA SCIMMIA

This is one of Naples' oldest gelaterie and reputedly some of the best ice cream in the city is served here, as well as exotic cakes and pastries. ✉ Piazza Trieste e Trento 54 ☎ 081 41 0322 ◷ Daily 7.30am–midnight; closed Wed ▢ 140, C9, C10, C24, C28, R3

OTRANTO

Stop in Vomero for one of their delicious ice creams. If you need more refreshment, try one of the beautiful ice cream-filled pastries. ✉ Via Scarlatti 78 ☎ 081 558 7498 ◷ Daily 9.30am–11pm; closed Wed ◉ Vanvitelli, Funicolare Piazza Fuga ▢ C28, C31, C32

PATISSERIE SCATURCHIO

Right on the busy piazza, this is one of Naples' most famous patisseries. They have superb *sfogliatelle*, as well as a range of other delicious pastries. ✉ Piazza San Domenico Maggiore 19 ☎ 081 551 6944 ◷ Daily 7.30am–8.30pm ◉ Dante ▢ E1, R4

REMY GELO

Over 30 types of ice cream are sold here, as well as several kinds of granita and frozen yoghurts. You can also buy prepared cakes and ice cream pastries. ✉ Via Ferdinando Galiani 29 ☎ 081 667 304 ◷ 9am–midnight ◉ Mergellina ▢ 140, C16, C24, R3

LA SFOGLIATELLA MARY

This is a local institution, so there are always queues waiting for their delicious pastries. As well as the traditional *sfogliatelle*, they also serve tempting rum babàs and cakes. ✉ Galleria Umberto I 66 ☎ 081 402 218 ◷ Mon 8–2.30, Tue–Sat 8am–8.30pm; closed Sun ◉ Funicolare Augusteo ▢ 140, C9, C10, C24, C28, R3

Art & Antiques

ANTICHITÀ
This shop specializes in buying and selling antique and modern paintings, objets d'art and gramophones, as well as silverware and furnishings.
✉ Via Foria 292 ☎ 081 291 383 🚍 4, C24, E5, R3

L'ARCHETTO
Top quality antiques only will be found at this elegant, sophisticated shop. The owners are very courteous and keen to help genuine buyers.
✉ Vico II Alabardieri 8 ☎ 081 402 647 🚇 Piazza Amedeo 🚍 C22, C24, C25, C28

LA BOTTEGA DELL'ARTE ANTICA
Ceramics, silver and paintings are all sold here, but they mainly specialize in furniture. There is a team of expert craftsmen on hand to carry out very accurate restoration.
✉ Via Arcoleo 25/27 ☎ 081 764 3170 🚍 C25, R3

DECAMANUS
In the hurly-burly of the Centro Storico, this elegant shop is a haven of peace. The beautiful 18th- and 19th-century furniture and pictures are spaciously set out, and there are some unusual ornaments, coral jewellery and glass.
www.decamanus.info ✉ Via Benedetto Croce 30/31 ☎ 081 551 8095 🚇 Dante 🚍 E1, E4

DEL PORTO
This fascinating shop carries tortoiseshell and coral items and jewellery, as well as a wider range of objects, such as porcelain.
✉ Via S Lucia 165 ☎ 081 764 0093 🚍 C25

EMANUELE CAPUANO
This pretty shop in Naples' bustling backstreets is the place to come for a painting of Naples. Many of them are in oils or watercolours, and some are relatively expensive, but it is fun just to browse.
✉ Via Santa Maria di Costantinopoli 52 ☎ 081 459 841

ERNESTO BOWINKEL
Apart from having a fascinating selection of prints and engravings, this shop is a treasure trove of collectables, statuettes, pottery and jewellery. All seem to have a story behind them, which the attentive staff will be all too pleased to tell you.
✉ Piazza dei Martiri 24 ☎ 081 764 4344 🚍 4, C24, E5, R3

ERRICO DI M & C
There are some gorgeous oriental carpets here, along with lamps and a variety of other antiques. Restorations are also undertaken.
✉ Via Carducci, 10 ☎ 081 414 524 🚇 Piazza Amedeo 🚍 C22, C24, C25, C28

FEBBRAIO FRANCO
Period furniture, some from the 18th century, is found at this elegant store, which is laden

SHOPPING AREAS

There are a number of areas in Naples where several antiques shops are grouped together. Find them around these and adjoining streets:
**Via Costantinopoli
Via Domenico Morelli
Vico Belledonne a Chiaia
Via Santa Lucia**.

71

ANTIQUES MARKET

The monthly **Fiera Antiquaria Napoletana** (➤ 57) is a great place for antiques lovers to find a bargain, and is held on the last Sunday of the month along Villa Comunale. It is full of paintings, prints (not all of them genuine), furniture, jewellery and other items whose curiousness exceeds their value.

with antiques. Staff can answer questions about taking items back home.
✉ Corso Vittorio Emanuele 758
☎ 081 667 707 🚇 Montesanto, Funicolare Montesanto 🚌 C16

FLORIDA
Beautiful glass objects are to be seen here, especially the candelabra. Take a special note of the fine paintings on glass.
✉ Via Domenico Morelli 13
☎ 081 764 3440 🚌 4, C24, E5, R3

FRATELLI MELLINO
This shop boasts an intriguing collection of pictures and other items inside or displayed on the steps outside. The witch sitting by the door is the shop's mascot.
✉ Piazzetta Nilo 18/19
☎ 081 552 0630 🚌 148, C55, C58, E1, R2

GARGIULO GIUSEPPE
One of the more famous antiques shops in Naples, with some unusual furniture, fabrics, objets d'art and traditional Neapolitan items.
✉ Via Imbriani 3313 ☎ 081 764 3474 🚌 C22, C25, R3

GUARRACINO CIRO
This well-established antiques shop, in an area full of antiques workshops, sells silverware and paintings, as well as some minor objects. Along with paintings and silver, they also specialize in furniture and furnishings.
✉ Piazza Carlo III 28/29
☎ 081 599 2000 🚌 14, 15, 47, 201, C5

MADAMALUNA
There is a wide variety of objects on sale here, from unusual antiques to fascinating objets d'art.
✉ Via Giuseppe Verdi 4 ☎ 081 401 990 🚌 140, C9, C10, C24, C28, R3

MARIO GIORDANO
There are some good reasonably priced reproductions of antique Neapolitan furniture here, together with ceramics and some interesting prints.
✉ Via Costantinopoli 100
☎ 081 210 946 🚇 Dante
🚌 201, C57, E1, R1, R4

M BRANDI
This is a very elegant shop that specializes in 18th-century antiques, and also has a selection of 19th-century furniture and paintings.
✉ Via Domenico Morelli 9/11
☎ 081 764 3882 🚌 4, C24, E5, R3

MIRLINUM
Silver, porcelain, Capodimonte ceramics and items from France, Germany and Britain are all at this elegant showroom, along with beautiful dried and silk flower arrangements.
✉ Via Giordano Bruno 154
☎ 081 761 3900
🚇 Mergellina 🚌 C16, C24, R3

SELEZIONE DEL DESIGN
This large shop, occupying two floors, has a superb collection of antique furnishings, some at quite reasonable prices.
✉ Via Benedetto Croce 16
☎ 081 551 7125 🚇 Dante
🚌 C36, E1, R4

Artisan Crafts

IL CANTUCCIO DELLA CERAMICA

Hidden away in a courtyard off the main street is a superb ceramics workshop, where a wide choice of cups, bowls, plates and dishes can be obtained. They also run short pottery courses.

✉ Via Benedetto Croce 38
☎ 081 552 5857 🚌 C36, E1

F.LLI CAPUANO

This crowded workshop makes some of the largest Christmas crèches around. The scenes are most elaborate, with several characters, as well as lights and working waterwheels.

✉ Via San Gregorio Armeno 28
☎ 081 551 9651 🚌 C36, E1

CRÈCHES GRAMENDOLA

In a street packed with traditional craftsmen, this workshop turns out a good variety of sizes and styles of Christmas crèche, many of which are now powered by electricity.

✉ Via San Gregorio Armeno 51
☎ 081 551 4899 🚇 Dante
🚌 E1, R4

GIUSEPPE FERRIGNO

Giuseppe and his son Marco carry on a family tradition of making Christmas crèches, religious scenes, statuettes of Pulcinella and more modern subjects. They have won awards the world over.
www.presepenapoletano.it/artigia ni/ferrigno/FERRIGN2.htm
✉ Via San Gregorio Armeno 10
☎ 081 552 3148 🚇 Dante
🚌 E1, R4

GIUSEPPE MILETTI

This is the place to come to have a musical instrument repaired, or to buy a mandolin. It is an Aladdin's cave of instruments of all kinds, including modern guitars.
✉ Via San Sebastiano 37
☎ 081 551 1801 🚇 Dante
🚌 E1, R4

MAESTRANZE NAPOLITANE

Raffaele Sorrentino, the head of this firm, makes wonderful objects in marble and precious stones. A showroom displays his work. He uses traditional techniques and makes reproductions as well as original pieces. He also restores damaged items.
www.maestranzenapoletane.com
✉ Via Conte di Ruvo 7/8
☎ 081 544 8836 🚇 Dante
🚌 201, C57, E1, R1, R4

OSPEDALE DELLE BAMBOLE

The dolls' hospital has been repairing beloved toys since 1800. It is worth looking inside to see some of the beautiful old dolls.
www.ospedaledellebambole.it
✉ Via San Biaggio dei Librai 81
🚌 148, C55, C58, R2

DI VIRGILLO

The family traditions of making figurines, models of shepherds, religious crafts and even wax baskets of fruit are maintained here in a cavern of treasures. Items range from the tiny to the huge.
✉ Via San Gregorio Armeno 18/20 ☎ 081 549 1642
🚇 Dante 🚌 E1, R4

CHRISTMAS CRÈCHES

The street of San Gregorio Armeno has, for centuries, been at the heart of a peculiarly Neapolitan tradition. Detailed models of religious scenes are created here for the decoration of people's homes. At Christmas time, shoppers from all over Italy descend to buy their *presepi* as they are called. They are on sale all year round, so it is possible to obtain examples at any time, thus avoiding the impenetrable crush at Christmas. Extraordinary craftsmanship can be seen in the workshops here, not all of which is restricted to traditional subjects. You will find models of footballers, for example, as well as food and animals, and there are plenty of potential souvenirs in every shop.

Fashion & Accessories

HIGH FASHION

Naples may not be in the same fashion league as Milan or Rome, but its citizens are still immensely style conscious. All the big names can be found in the city, and many world-famous names are based here. Tramontano, for example, sells from New York to Japan, but his manufacturing base is here. The designer Alessandro Dell'Acqua was born and trained in Naples, and so was the city's most famous designer, Alessio Visone. Indeed, Salvatore Ferragamo, shoemaker to the stars, was born close to Naples.

ALDO TRAMONTANO

Wonderful, prized hand-made leather bags, wallets, belts and suitcases emanate from here. Look for the trademark wolf's head on the belts.
www.aldotramontano.it ✉ Via Chiaia 143/145 ☎ 081 41 4837 🚌 4, C24, E5, R3

COIN

This moderately priced department store has smart clothes for men, women and children, as well as fashion accessories. It also sells kitchenware.
www.coin.it ✉ Via Scarlatti 94/98 ☎ 081 578 0111 🚇 Vanvitelli, Funicolare Piazza Fuga, Funicolare Via Morghen 🚌 C24, C27

EDDY MONETTI

The classic menswear store in the city for every well-dressed gentleman. (There is a companion shop for ladies at Piazzetta Santa Caterina 8.)
✉ Via dei Mille 45 ☎ 081 407 064 🚇 Piazza Amedeo 🚌 C22, C24, C25, C28

EUGENIO MARINELLA

This establishment has been in business for over 80 years and has been patronized by nobility and the wealthy. It is the best place in the city to buy a tie, but they also sell other smart menswear.
www.marinellanapoli.it ✉ Riviera di Chiaia 287 ☎ 081 764 4214 🚌 4, C24, E5, R3

MAX MARA

A friendly place in which to try some of the latest styles from this international name. Many are informal, and they also sell accessories and sunglasses.
✉ Piazza Trieste e Trento 51 ☎ 081 406 242 🚌 C25, R3

MELINOI AND THE CHINESE COMPANY

For individual and stylish women's clothes, head for this unusual shop. Many items are by young, up-and-coming designers, and there is plenty of vibrant choice.
www.tuttosunapoli.net/melinoi/ ✉ Via Benedetto Croce 34 ☎ 081 552 1204 🚇 Dante 🚌 E1, R4

PRADA

The chic, minimalist clothes store has a presence in this trendy area of the city, along with other international fashion brands.
www.prada.it ✉ Via Calabritto 9 ☎ 081 764 1323 🚌 4, C24, E5, R3

SALVATORE FERRAGAMO

This large and stylish store takes up one side of Piazza dei Martiri. The men's shop is next door to the ladies'. The clothes and accessories are fashionable, yet practical.
www.ferragamo.com ✉ Piazza dei Martiri 56/60 ☎ 081 415 454 🚌 4, C24, E5, R3

YIEN

Individual shoes, jewellery and accessories that are not outrageously expensive and have a stylish practicality.
✉ Via Alabardieri 40 ☎ 081 41 2770 🚌 4, C24, E5, R3

Food & Wine

ANTICA PANETTERIA

A small shop, but one filled with a great variety of different types of bread, and it will be difficult to leave without buying some.

✉ Via Pignasecca 20 🚇 Montesanto, Funicolare Montesanto 🚌 24, E2, R1, R4

ARFÉ

This is one of the most prestigious food shops in Naples, and stocks a tremendous variety of cheeses, pasta, and cooked dishes.

✉ Strada Santa Theresa a Chiaia 45 ☎ 081 41 1822 🚌 C24, C25, C26, C27, C28

BOTTEGA DEL CASARO

It is hard to believe there could be as many different kinds of pasta as can be found in this small shop. Find some unusual examples to take home.

✉ Via Mezzocanone 145 ☎ 081 552 2656 🚇 Dante 🚌 E1, R4

DOLCE IDEA

Some amazing chocolate creations are sold here, and it is difficult to resist trying a few examples before buying. There are two other branches: in Vomero and near Piazza del Plebiscito.

✉ Via S Liborio 2 ☎ 081 420 3090 🚌 24, E2, R1, R4

ENOTECA BELLEDONNE

The owners are very knowledgeable about wine and are happy to discuss it with you. This can be a very rewarding way to find the best of the local wines, or to seek out something more esoteric.

✉ Vico delle Belledonne a Chiaia 18 ☎ 081 403 162 🚌 C22, C25, R3

ENOTECA DEL BUON BERE

This place stocks a very good selection of Italian and international wines. It is also possible to buy food here, such as pâté, cold meat and cakes.

✉ Via M Turchi 13 ☎ 081 764 7843 🚌 C25

GAY ODIN

A most tempting range of chocolate products in all shapes, sizes and wrappings is available at this famous chocolatier. There are seven other branches in the city.

www.gay-odin.it ✉ Via Toledo 427/428 ☎ 081 551 3491 🚇 Dante 🚌 210, C57, E1, R1, R4

LIMONE

The plentiful lemons of the area are transformed into the delicious liqueur *limoncello*. This shop sells several varieties of this drink, as well as many other lemon-tasting products.

www.limoncellodinapoli.it ✉ Piazza S Gaetano 72 (San Paolo Maggiore) ☎ 081 29 9429 🚇 Dante 🚌 E1, R4

PESCHERIA AZZURRA

Fresh fish is a vital part of Neapolitan life, and this sparkling shop with its blue tiles has one of the best displays of the different kinds on offer.

✉ Via Portamedina 4 ☎ 081 551 3733 🚇 Montesanto, Funicolare Montesanto 🚌 24, E2, R1, R4

MARKETS

Fresh food is undoubtedly best purchased from one of the city markets. Even if you do not buy anything, the spectacle and bustle are experiences in themselves. The good markets to visit for food are **Porta Nolana** and **Pignasecca** (➤ 57).

LOCAL DELICACIES

There are so many delicious foods in Naples it can be hard to choose which to take home. Here are some suggestions:

Cheese – Mozzarella was first made near Naples from the milk of water buffaloes. It is now made from cows' milk and can be found in many guises. Smoked mozzarella is particularly tasty. Other cheeses from the region are *scamorza* and *cacciocavallo*.

Wine – The best red wine from the region is Taurasi, which is rich and strong. For white wine, Lachryma Christi del Vesuvio is full bodied and dry, while a more fruity white wine is Falanghina dei Campi Flegrei.

Meat – Salame di Napoli has a smoky, spicy taste and is still made locally using traditional methods.

Biscuits – A traditional local delicacy is the *taralli*, a crunchy biscuit with a salt and pepper taste.

Books, Prints & Stationery

WRITERS ON NAPLES

One of the best-known modern books about Naples is Norman Lewis' wartime diary *Naples '44*, which records both the horrors and the lighter moments of the Allied occupation of the city. Another good history is *Modern Naples* by John Santore. Robert Harris' *Pompei* is an excellent account of the disaster there. Anna Maria Ortese, one of Italy's foremost female writers and poets lived in Naples for many years. Several of her books are translated into English. For a lighter read, Michael Dibden's *Cosi Fan Tutti* (1997) is a detective story set in Naples.

CASA DELLA PENNA

A very well-established shop near the university, which stocks an excellent variety of pens, from the practical everyday kind to fashion pens from top designers.
✉ Corso Umberto I 88 ☎ 081 204 763 🚍 148, C55, E1, R2

COLONNESE BOOKSHOP

A literary establishment in Naples, this shop has intriguing old and new books as well as prints, postcards and other stationery items. There are also literary events.
✉ Via San Pietro a Maiella 32/33 ☎ 081 459 858 🚇 Dante 🚍 E1, E4

ERNESTO BOWINKEL

The main interest here is the large selection of prints, but there are a few books as well, together with some antiques and jewellery.
✉ Piazza dei Martiri 24 ☎ 081 764 4344 🚍 4, C24

ETTORE SMITH

Paper and card of all sizes and hues is stocked in abundance at this crowded shop, where original and everyday items can be found at good prices.
✉ Via Benedetto Croce 52 ☎ 081 551 6989 🚇 Dante 🚍 E1, E4

EVALUNA

This charming shop has chairs scattered around for quiet reading, and collections of prints as well as books. It has a particular reputation for holding a wide range of women's interest titles.
✉ Piazza Bellini 72 ☎ 081 44 5759 🚇 Dante 🚍 E1, E4

FELTRINELLI

The biggest and best modern bookshop in the city has three floors and a coffee shop. There is a good selection of English-language books, as well as magazines, stationery and music. They also host literary and cultural events.
✉ Via Santa Caterina a Chiaia 23 ☎ 081 240 5411 🚍 4, C24, E5, R3

INTRA MOENIA

Linked to the literary café of the same name in Piazza Bellini (➤ 80), this attractive little shop (in a courtyard off the main street) stocks interesting books and cards.
www.intramoenia.it
✉ Benedetto Croce 38 ☎ 081 290 720 🚇 Dante 🚍 E1, E4

LIBRERIA MONDADORI

Incongruously placed in the middle of the old shops in Centro Storico, this modern bookshop has a reasonable range of popular books, some local books and a few English-language titles.
✉ Via Benedetto Croce 28 ☎ 081 420 3308 🚇 Dante 🚍 E1, E4

PIRONTI

There are several bookshops, including branches of Pironti, in the parade along Piazza Cavour, where modern and some second-hand books are stocked in large numbers.
✉ Piazza Cavour 70 ☎ 081 457 391 🚇 Piazza Cavour 🚍 14, 15, 47, 201, C5

Jewellers

ARTE IN ORO
This charming shop in Centro Storico sells a range of antique and unique items, including reproductions of Roman jewellery.
✉ Via Benedetto Croce 20 ☎ 081 551 6980 🚋 E1, R4

BARTOLI
This is one of the best jewellers in the city, and it has some superb watches, as well as a huge choice of sparkling rings and brooches.
✉ Via Francesco Cilea 67/71 ☎ 081 560 0808 🚋 Cilea, Vanvitelli, Funicolare Piazza Fuga 🚋 C24, C27

F.LLE ESPOSITO
Located in the heart of the city's traditional jewellery quarter, this shop specializes in beautiful gold jewellery, which they have been making for years. These and their silver designs are fine examples of the art.
✉ Via Giovanni Manna 19/21 ☎ 081 553 8938 🚋 148, C55, E1, R2

GALLERIA AUREA
For years stars of stage and screen have bought their jewellery from this famous shop, which has a dazzling selection of ritzy earrings and necklaces.
✉ Galleria Umberto I 171 ☎ 081 417 876 🚋 Funicolare Augusteo 🚋 140, C9, C10, C24, C28, R3

GALLOTTA
Unless you are very wealthy, this exclusive shop will be merely a place in which to dream and marvel at the beautiful creations produced here over many years.
✉ Via Chiaia 139 ☎ 081 421 164 🚋 Funicolare Augusteo 🚋 4, C24, E5, R3

GIOIELLI CARAMANNA
One of the more expensive shops in a fashionable area, this place has some beautiful modern jewellery and very unusual designs.
✉ Via Calabritto 22 ☎ 081 764 9875 🚋 4, C24, E5, R3

GIOIELLERIA CASO
Beautiful pieces of coral jewellery sit side by side with a collection of antique jewellery and silver, and a great selection of cameos in this charming shop in Centro Storico.
✉ Piazza San Domenico Maggiore 16 ☎ 081 551 6733 🚋 Dante 🚋 E1, R4

GIOIELLERIA PRESTA
Superb craftsmanship in coral carving is one example of the top-quality work carried out at this shop in the jewellery quarter. They are also fine goldsmiths.
✉ Via Antonio Scialoia 2/10 ☎ 081 554 5282 🚋 148, C55, E1, R2

VENTRELLA
One of the most famous contemporary jewellery designers in Naples displays some of his highly original work at this fascinating shop. He can also design one-off pieces to order.
www.ventrella.it ✉ Via Carlo Poerio 11 ☎ 081 764 3173 🚋 C22, C25, R3

CORAL JEWELLERY
One of the largest coral beds in the world lies off the coast of Naples, and coral work has been carried out in the area (principally around Torre del Greco) since the 15th century. The red hue of coral has had mystical significance through the ages. In ancient mythology it represented the blood from the decapitated head of Medusa. Christians saw it as representative of Christ's blood. In any event red coral has always been in much demand, and reached the peak of popularity during the reign of the Bourbons. It is still much prized today, and examples of superb craftsmanship can be seen in many of the city's jewellers.

Interior Design, Fabrics & Ceramics

DEPARTMENT STORES

Good-quality household items can be obtained from the department stores in the city. The main ones are:
Coin (✉ Via Scarlatti 88/100 ☎ 081 578 0111)
Rinascente (✉ Via Toledo 343 ☎ 081 411 511)
Upim (✉ Via Nisco 11 ☎ 081 417 520).

D'ANDREA

Established in 1835, this shop has a reputation as one of the best places to buy linen, and has an excellent range of material, tablecloths and eiderdowns (comforters).
✉ Via Santa Brigida 7 ☎ 081 552 5538 🚌 C25, R3

BACHELITE

A wide collection of unusual and attractive items draws people to this unique shop, which specializes in 20th-century objects.
✉ Vico Belledonne a Chiaia 2 ☎ 081 411 860 🚌 C22, C25, R3

BASSETTI

There are sheets, pillowcases and other items of household linen at this branch of Italy's foremost producer of such items. There is another shop at Via Scarlatti 209D.
✉ Piazza Trieste e Trento 44 ☎ 081 411 742 🚌 C25, R3

BRAENDLI

This small shop in the Centro Storico stocks the best quality Italian wallpapers and fabrics. There is a wide choice of materials, and the staff are most helpful.
✉ Via Cisterna dell'Olio 5A/5B ☎ 081 552 0196 🚇 Dante 🚌 24, 201, C57, E1, R1, R4

CHIAIA DESIGN

Attractive modern designs (ranging from glass and ceramics to furniture) from a variety of designers can be seen at this smart shop in Chiaia.

www.chiaiainteriordesign.it
✉ Via Riviera di Chiaia 257 ☎ 081 245 7408 🚌 C22, C25, R3

COLLECTION

You can get fashionable fabrics and accessories here for running up your own creations, from names such as Armani and Valentino.
✉ Vico Belledonne a Chiaia 15 ☎ 081 419 414 🚌 C22, C25, R3

COMPAGNIA DELLA CASA

This bright, modern store keeps an affordable and attractively laid out collection of smartly designed items for the home. Lots of choice.
✉ Via Toledo 294/295 ☎ 081 415 459 🚋 Funicolare Augusteo 🚌 201, C25, C57, E3, E5, R3

CROFF

Unusual and irresistible objects for the home are specially made for this shop by local craftsmen.
✉ Via Armando Diaz 32 ☎ 081 552 3983 🚌 201, C25, C57, E3

DOMUS

This shop sells handcrafted Persian carpets of all sizes, in an atmosphere of an Arabian souk.
✉ Via dei Mille 1/9 ☎ 081 404 809 🚇 Piazza Amedeo 🚌 C22, C24, C25, C28

ESPACE MONTEOLIVETO 11

This very small studio displays unusual glass and ceramic pieces from individual artists and craftsmen, and you are bound to find something unique.

✉ Piazza Monteoliveto 11
☎ 081 1956 9414 🚌 201, C57

FRETTE

Unashamedly luxurious, the sheets, towels and linen in this shop are the finest in the city and are well worth seeking out for that special purchase.

✉ Via dei Mille 2 ☎ 081 418 728 🚌 C22, C24, C25, C28

GIALLO NAPOLI

Here you will find a wonderful stock of ceramic urns and bowls, terracotta kitchenware and striking blue Sicilian objets d'art.

✉ Via Carlo Poerio 114 ☎ 081 764 0622 🚌 C22, C25, R3

MARCELLO D'AMATO

This small shop in a backstreet off Via Monteoliveto makes beautiful glass lamps, mirrors and boxes, all by hand, and to order.

✉ Via Donnalbina 37 ☎ 081 251 4091 🚌 201, C57

MARIO BOTTIGLIERI DESIGN

An abundant and exotic range of things all based on a Roman theme can be found here. Choose from golden goblets, headwear and ancient statues, most of them highly impractical.

✉ Vico Belledonne a Chiaia 20
☎ 081 401 197 🚌 C22, C25, R3

LA MURRINA

There are wonderful pieces of blown glass from Murano (near Venice) available here.

Vivid and contemporary, each piece of design is unique.

www.lamurrina.com ✉ Via San Carlo 18 ☎ 081 406 452
🚌 C25, R3

NABIS

Art nouveau and art deco furniture and household decorations are the theme of this interesting shop, where many unusual items can be found.

✉ Via Cavallerizza a Chiaia 52
☎ 081 422 493 🚌 C22, C25, R3

NOVELLI ARREDAMENTO

In an attractive setting on Piazza Amedeo, this shop has some very inventive designs and smart modern furniture. A browse around the shop will undoubtedly be very rewarding.

✉ Piazza Amedeo 21/22
☎ 081 413 233 Ⓜ Piazza Amedeo 🚌 C22, C24, C25, C28

LA RIGGIOLA NAPOLETANA

Tiles of all kinds, many of them beautifully decorated, can be found in this workshop, tucked away off Via Monteoliveto. The staff are most helpful.

✉ Via Donalbina 22 ☎ 081 551 8022 🚌 201, C57, R1

LA VETRINA

The splendid Palazzo Filomarino, built in 1512, is home to this delightful shop, which sells a variety of ceramics, ornaments and gifts.

✉ Via Benedetto Croce 12
☎ 081 551 9313 Ⓜ Dante
🚌 E1, R4

ITALIAN DESIGN IN THE HOME

The byword for smart design is Italian, and a visit to Naples is a wonderful opportunity to pick up some pieces to enhance the style of your home. The designers to look out for are Minotti and Zanotte for furniture and Frette for linen. Gadgets designed with a sense of fun come from Alessi, while Piazza make smart cutlery. The big names are also moving into this field and Armani, Versace and Bulgari have all produced ranges of textiles and dinnerware to rival the others.

Bars by Night

MORE BARS

Naples' nightlife is very lively and there are plenty of places to enjoy yourself in the evening. Among them are **Rock Café** (✉ Piazzetta Ascensione 26/27 ☎ 081 404 476), a small, friendly, bar up a narrow street just off the waterfront; **La Scalinatella** (✉ Via San Pasquale a Chiaia 51 ☎ 081 251 2478), and **Las Tapas Bar** (✉ Piazzetta del Nilo 36 ☎ 333 414 9322), which does not sell tapas, but is an agreeable place for a late-night drink.

LE BAR

The buzzing atmosphere in the Borgo Marinari area is best enjoyed from the seats of this bar, where you can watch the world go by while enjoying a drink and some live music.
✉ Via Eldorado 7, Borgo Marinari ☎ 081 764 5722
🚍 C25, R3

ENOTECA BELLEDONNE

Functioning as a wine shop in the day, this place turns into a popular bar in the evenings. There is, naturally, a good choice of wines, and this is a good way to try a few before ordering them. Other drinks are also served.
✉ Vico delle Belledonne a Chiaia 18 ☎ 081 40 3162
🕐 Wine shop: daily 9–2, 4.30–8; wine bar: 8pm–2am
🚍 C22, C25, R3

INTRA MOENIA

This famous literary establishment is also a charming bar in an attractive piazza, where cocktails and drinks of all kinds are served, as well as teas and some light snacks.
www.intramoenia.it ✉ Piazza Bellini 70 ☎ 081 290 720
🕐 Daily 10am–2am 🚇 Dante
🚍 201, C57, E1, R1, R4

KINKY BAR

The DJ here plays mainly rock and house music, and the small bar is always full. So much so that the clientele frequently spills out on to the street. The beers are good and the place is friendly.

✉ Via Cisterno dell'Olio 21
☎ 081 552 1571 🕐 Daily 10.30pm–3am; closed Jun–Sep
🚇 Dante 🚍 24, 201, C57, E1, R1, R4

LONTANO DA DOVE

A bookshop during the day and a small bar in the evening with live music. A meeting point for artists and writers, it also puts on theatre and shows films.
www.lontanodadove.com ✉ Via Bellini 3 ☎ 081 549 4304
🚇 Dante 🚍 24, 201, C57, E1, R1, R4

S'MOVE

A very smooth bar with comfortable furniture and plenty of space. Even so, it can get quite crowded. It is a friendly bar and a smart place to be seen.
✉ Vico dei Sospiri ☎ 081 764 5813 🚍 C9, C10, C24, C25, R3

SUPERFLY

A small bar with only a few stools, but the jazz played by the DJ is worth squeezing in for. There are also photographic exhibitions here from time to time.
✉ Via Cisterna dell'Olio 11
☎ 347 127 2178 🕐 Tue–Sun 7pm–3am; closed Jul–Sep
🚇 Dante 🚍 24, 201, C57, E1, R1, R4

TEMPIO DI BACCO

A wine cellar converted into a sparkling bar, with fluorescent lights and tables suspended by chains from the ceiling. A very chilled place.
✉ Vico San Domenico Maggiore 1 ☎ 081 294 354
🚇 Dante 🚍 24, 201, C57, E1, R1, R4

Clubs & Dance Bars

ARET' A' PALM

A noisy city club, this has a stylish long bar and interior. The DJ plays jazz and rock music, and there is seating in the piazza for when it is busy.
✉ Piazza Santa Maria la Nova 14 ☎ 339 848 6949
🕐 Mon–Fri 10am–2pm, Sat and Sun 6pm–2am 🚌 C25, R1, R3

CAFÉ CANTANTE

This popular club attracts a young crowd to enjoy pop, rap, soul and house music until the early hours. There is a bar with a wide range of beers and spirits.
✉ Via Palepoli 8 ☎ 081 240 5068 🕐 Wed–Sun 10.30pm–3.30am 🚌 C25

EL CHICO

A Mexican-themed club, where tequila slammers are all the rage and nachos and tortillas soak up the alcohol. Crowds arrive after work, and dancing goes on till late.
✉ Rampe di San Antonio a Posillipo 45 ☎ 081 662 823
🕐 Daily 4pm–2am
🚉 Mergellina 🚌 C16, C24, R3

LORNA DOONÈ

This sophisticated club has a small dance floor and can get crowded, but it is a good place to watch Naples' smart set.
✉ Vico Satriano 10 ☎ 339 266 4786 🕐 Tue–Sun 7pm–3.30am; closed Aug 🚌 C9, C10, C24, C25, R3

LA MELA

A long-established city nightclub, this is a fashionable place to be seen. There is a resident DJ who keeps the smart customers entertained.

✉ Via delle Mille 40 ☎ 081 410 270 🕐 Thu–Sun midnight–4am 🚉 Piazza Amedeo 🚌 C22, C24, C25, C28

MY WAY

An atmospheric club carved into the rock, near the fashionable shops in Chiaia. The DJs play rock and techno music to a young crowd.
✉ Via Cappella Vecchia 30 ☎ 081 245 1887 🚌 C9, C10, C24, C25, R3

QUEEN VICTORIA

A spacious, modern venue in Chiaia. There are occasional visits by blues, jazz and pop bands, and the DJs play house music when there are no live groups.
✉ Via dei Mille ☎ 081 422 334 🕐 Wed–Sun 7pm–2am
🚉 Piazza Amedeo 🚌 C22, C24, C25, C28

VELVET

A popular club, which gets crowded for major attractions. A DJ plays for much of the time, but there are regular live acts. There is plenty of room for dancing.
✉ Via Cisterna dell'Olio 11 ☎ 347 810 7328 🕐 Tue–Thu 11pm–4am, Fri and Sat 11pm–6am; closed Jun–Sep 🚉 Dante 🚌 24, 201, C57, E1, R1, R4

VIBES BAR

Close to the Centro Storico and the university, this popular bar has a lively atmosphere, and often has live music.
✉ Largo San Giovanni Maggiore 26/27 ☎ 081 551 3984
🕐 Mon–Fri 8pm–3am, Sat and Sun 7pm–3am 🚉 Dante
🚌 24, 201, C57, E1

CLUBS OUT OF TOWN

A great deal of the club scene in Naples takes place out of town. The clubs are usually not easy to get to by public transport, so taxis will be needed. Here's a club selection:

Jasay (✉ Via Marina, opposite municipal parking ☎ 081 553 9189)
Kiss Kiss (a disco on two floors ✉ Via Sgambati 47, ☎ 081 546 6566)
Sly Discobar (☎ Via Orazio 75 ☎ 081 664 048)
Tongue (✉ Via Manzoni 207 ☎ 081 769 0800)
Up Stroke (one of the clubs in the Arenile area, rather like a 24-hour holiday resort ✉ Via Coroglio 128 ☎ 081 570 8992)
Verve (✉ Via Petrarca 101, Posillipo ☎ 081 575 4882)
Virgilio (gay club ✉ Via Tito Lucrezio Caro 6 ☎ 338 345 9007).

81

Live Music

NEAPOLIS ROCK FESTIVAL

Every year in July Naples hosts one of Italy's best rock festivals, and the only one on the coast. The aim is to create a 'Woodstock by the sea'. It has been going since 1997, and has attracted some of the biggest names in international rock and pop as well as the best of the Italian and Neapolitan groups. The festival is held on two stages over two days in the Italsider area around Bagnoli, and the focus is Piazza Bagnoli (✉ 49 Italsider di Bagnoli, Via Coroglio ☎ 081 240 4276). For details of the schedule, see their website www.neapolis.it, and also www.whatsonwhen.com.

BOURBON STREET

Across the road from Murat, this popular club is dedicated to local jazz. It is quite spacious and has a bright, fashionable atmosphere. www.bourbonstreetclub.it ✉ Via Bellini 52 ☎ 328 068 7221 🕐 Tue–Sun 9pm–3am; closed Jul and Aug 🚇 Dante 🚌 C57, E1, R1, R4

ISTITUTO GRENOBLE

World-class jazz musicians can occasionally be heard at concerts held in the auditorium of this university outpost. Watch the local press for details. ✉ Via Francesco Crispi 86 ☎ 333 700 5230 🚇 Piazza Amedeo 🚌 C24, C27

MURAT CLUB

A slightly older crowd patronizes this friendly club. There are some great cocktails and sometimes light snacks. Live jazz is played, particularly on weekends. ✉ Via Bellini 8 ☎ 081 544 5919 🕐 Wed–Sun 7pm–2am 🚇 Dante 🚌 C57, E1, R1, R4

NOTTING HILL

A cavernous cellar with the stage at the far end, it can be hard to get to the front of this club. You can hear touring British and other international groups, as well as local musicians and bands from other parts of Italy. ✉ Piazza Dante 88A ☎ 335 587 0247 🕐 Tue–Sat 10.30pm–4am; closed Jun–Sep 🚇 Dante 🚌 24, C57, E1, R1, R4

OTTO JAZZ

This is the top place in Naples to hear jazz. Long established and with an excellent reputation, it attracts musicians from all over the world, as well as local players. The atmosphere is relaxed, and the bar sometimes sells food. ✉ Salita Cariati 23 ☎ 081 551 3765 🕐 Fri–Sun 11pm–2am; closed Jul and Aug 🚇 Funicolare Corso Vittorio Emanuele 🚌 C16, C24

PALAPARTENOPE

A huge tent, out of town at Edenlandia, this is the largest venue in Naples for major touring bands and individual musicians. Check the website for details of forthcoming gigs. www.palapartenope.it ✉ Via Barbagallo, Edenlandia ☎ 081 570 0008 🚇 Cumana di Agnano, Motta Zoo 🚇 Cavalleggeri D'Aosta 🚌 C9

SLOVENLY

This is a Centro Storico rock 'n' roll club that features bands from all over the world. It also spotlights new wave, '80s pop and electropop bands. www.slovenly.com ✉ Vico San Geronimo 24 ☎ 081 552 6108 🚇 Dante 🚌 E1, R4

TUNNEL AMEDEO

Originally a cinema, this enterprising place now shows cabaret, drama and jazz music as well as films. Watch for their posters around the city. ✉ Via G Martucci 69 ☎ 081 680 266 🚇 Piazza Amedeo 🚌 C24, C27

Opera, Ballet & Classical Music

CHIESA EVANGELICA LUTERANA DI NAPOLI

Classical concerts take place in this Chiaia church in the spring and autumn. There are also music competitions.
www.lutero.org ✉ Via Carlo Poerio 5 ☎ 081 663 2070
🚇 C22, C25, R3

CHIESA DI SANTA CATERINA DA SIENA

They specialize in baroque music here, and there are concerts by Centro di Musica Antiqua Pietà dei Turchini. Turquoise (*turchini*) was worn by the choirboys in the original school.
www.turchini.it ✉ Via Santa Caterina da Siena 38 ☎ 081 40 2395/081 409 628 🎫 Box office 1 hour before performances
🚇 Funicolare Corso Vittorio Emanuele 🚇 C16, C24

CONSERVATORIO SAN PIETRO A MAIELLA

This 14th-century convent houses one of the country's most famous conservatories. There are two concert halls, one for orchestral performances and the other for chamber recitals.
✉ Via San Pietro a Maiella 15 ☎ 081 459 255 🚇 R1

TEATRO AUGUSTEO

Big musical productions are featured here, as well as dance, song and comedy, with famous stars, and sometimes English-language plays.
www.teatroaugusteo.com
✉ Piazzetta Duca D'Aosta ☎ 081 414 243 🎫 Box office Tue–Sat 10.30–1.30, 4.30–7.30
🚇 Funicolare Augusteo
🚇 C25, C57, E3, E5, R3

TEATRO DELLE PALME

This plain, wooden auditorium (which also doubles as a cinema) is home to some classical music concerts produced by the Associazione Scarlatti. Local press and posters can also give some information.
www.napoli.com/assocscarlatti
✉ Via Vetriera 12 ☎ 081 418 134 🚇 Piazza Amedeo
🚇 C25

TEATRO DIANA

Classical music concerts are regularly held here, but the schedule also includes comedies, musical shows and drama, generally in Italian.
www.teatrodiana.it ✉ Via Luca Giordano 6 ☎ 081 556 7527
🎫 Box office daily 11–1.30, 4.30–8 🚇 Vanvitelli, Funicolare Piazza Fuga 🚇 C24, C27

TEATRO POLITEAMA

A highly respected concert hall, with links to several of Europe's leading opera houses. There are chamber operas and classical recitals here, as well as contemporary works put on for Teatro di San Carlo.
✉ Via Monte di Dio 80 ☎ 081 764 5001 🎫 Box office Mon–Sat 10.30–1.30 🚇 C22, E3

TEATRO SAN CARLO

One of the best opera houses in Italy, it has a truly sumptuous velvet and gilt interior. World-class performers come here, and performances are often fully booked.
www.teatrosancarlo.it ✉ Via San Carlo 98F ☎ 081 797 2331 🎫 Box office 10–3; closed Aug 🚇 C25, R2, R3

MUSICAL LEGACY

Naples has a long history of classical music, and in the 17th century it was at the heart of operatic development in Europe. The city's most celebrated composer is Alessandro Scarlatti, whose son Domenico Scarlatti was also born here and went on to become another great composer. Other baroque composers who studied in the city were Cimarosa and Pergolesi. Later, Mendelssohn composed his 'Italian' Symphony in Naples. For a time, Rossini was musical and artistic director at Teatro di San Carlo. The most famous musician associated with the city, though, must be Caruso. He was born in Naples in 1873, the 15th out of 21 children. Although he sang all over the world, his heart was always in the place of his birth, and he returned to the city, where he died in 1921 to universal mourning.

FONDAZIONE NAPOLITANO

This organization arranges concerts of classical music in various venues around the city, from churches and theatres to hotel salons. For information about the schedule, see **www.inaples.it/eng/eventimusicali.htm**.

Theatres

BOOKING TICKETS

Tickets for the most popular shows will go quickly. The following ticket agencies will help to smooth the path:
Concerteria (✉ Via Schipa 21 ☎ 081 761 1221)
Il Botteghino (✉ Via Pitloo 3 ☎ 081 556 4684)
MC Teatroemusica (Via Giulio Palermo 124 ☎ 081 546 2264).

CINEMAS

Film is very popular in Naples and there are some good cinemas ranging from the popular to art house. The major ones are:
Academy Astra (✉ Via Mezzocannone ☎ 081 552 0713)
Adriano (✉ Via Monteoliveto ☎ 081 551 3005)
Agorà (✉ Via Guanti Nuovi ☎ 081 552 4893)
Alcione (✉ Via Lomonaco ☎ 081 406 375)
Ambasciatori (✉ Via Crispi ☎ 081 761 3128)
Delle Palme (✉ Via Vetriera ☎ 081 418 134)
Empire (✉ Via Giordani ☎ 081 681 900)
Filangieri (✉ Via Filangieri ☎ 081 251 2408)
Metropolitan (✉ Via Chiaia ☎ 081 417 022)
Modernissimo (✉ Via Cisterna dell'Olio 59 ☎ 081 551 1247)
President (✉ Via Campanella ☎ 081 682 114).

GALLERIA TOLEDO

An exciting, modern venue, where experimental work is performed. They also have a cinema for avant-garde films.
www.galleriatoledo.com ✉ Via Concezione a Montecalvario 36 ☎ 081 42 5037/081 42 5824 🚇 Montesanto, Funicolare Augusteo 🚌 E2

SAN CARLUCCIO

This small, intimate venue offers contemporary and experimental drama and music, with more conventional productions occasionally.
www.teatrosancarluccio.com ✉ Via San Pasquale a Chiaia 49 ☎ 081 405 000 🕐 Tue–Sun 10–1.30, 4–8 🚇 Piazza Amedeo 🚌 C22, C25, R3

TEATRO BELLINI

The beautifully gilded restoration makes a grand setting for musicals and main-stream shows, as well as operas and ballets.
www.teatrobellini.it ✉ Via Conte di Ruvo 14/19 ☎ 081 549 9688 🕐 Tue–Sat 10.30–1, 4.30–6 🚇 Dante 🚌 201, C57, E1, R1, R4

TEATRO MERCADANTE

This place has been going strong since 1779 and some of Italy's leading performers and writers come here.
www.caspi.it/mercadante ✉ Piazza Municipio 1 ☎ 081 5511 9188 🕐 Mon–Fri 10.30–1, 5.30–7.30 🚌 C25, R3

TEATRO NUOVO

This experimental locale puts on high-quality productions of contemporary drama. Watch for posters locally.
www.nuovoteatronuovo.it ✉ Via Montecalvario 16 ☎ 081 406 062/081 425 958 🕐 Mon–Fri 5–7, Sat 11–1 🚇 Montesanto, Funicolare Augusteo 🚌 E2

TEATRO LE NUVOLE

This place for children out at Edenlandia has a variety of shows and workshops, some with a science theme. They also run projects with other venues in the city.
www.lenuvole.com ✉ Viale Kennedy 26, Edenlandia ☎ 081 239 5653 🚇 Cavalleggeri D'Aosta 🚌 C9

TEATRO SANNAZARO

Many famous Neapolitan actors and singers have performed at this traditional playhouse, and most performances are in Italian.
www.teatrosannazaro.it ✉ Via Chiaia 157 ☎ 081 403 827/081 411 723 🕐 Box office Tue–Sat 10–1.30, 4–8 🚌 C22, C25, R3

TEATRO TINTADIROSSO

This tiny venue in the Marigliano Palace has a charming roof garden. The performances are experimental, with the occasional film.
✉ Via San Biagio dei Librai 39 ☎ 081 790 1270 🚇 Dante 🚌 E1, R4

TEATRO TRIANON

Neapolitan song is revered in this beautifully restored playhouse, where traditions are respected.
www.teatrotrianon.it ✉ Piazza Calenda 9 ☎ 081 225 8285 🚇 Piazza Garibaldi 🚌 R2

Sport

ARCO FELICE GOLF CLUB
There is one nine-hole course at Pozzuoli, and another, Volturno Golf, 35km (22 miles) north.
✉ Via Campiglione II 118, Arco Felice ☎ 081 421 479
🕐 Wed–Mon 8–dusk, Tue pm only 🚇 Pozzuoli 🚋 Cumana train

BAGNO ELANA
South of Mergellina is a small bay with a beach, sunbeds and parasols. Admission charge.
✉ Via Posillipo 14 ☎ 081 575 5058 🚌 140

BOWLING OLTREMARE
A modern bowling alley with 20 lanes, near the Edenlandia funfair.
✉ Viale J. F. Kennedy, Fuorigrotta ☎ 081 624 444
🕐 Daily 9am–2am 🚋 Campi Flegrei 🚌 C9, C10

CIRCOLO DEL REMO E DELLA VELA ITALIA
This sailing club helps those (of any ability) who want to take lessons.
www.crvitalia.it ✉ Banchina Santa Lucia ☎ 081 764 6393
🚌 C25

CLUB ALPINO ITALIANO
This club can give you information about Naples walking excursions.
✉ Via Passaggio Castello dell'Ovo ☎ 081 764 5343
🕐 Tue and Fri 7pm–9pm
🚌 140

COLLANA
An indoor swimming pool in Vomero, with a sundeck and a gym.
✉ Via Rossini ☎ 081 560 1988 🕐 Open Jul and Aug
🚋 Cilea

IPPODROMO DI AGNANO
The famous racetrack in Naples is in Agnano, north of Bagnoli. There are eight tracks and events are held regularly.
✉ Via Ippodromo Agnano
☎ 081 570 2610 🚋 Bagnoli

LIDO MARECHIARO
To reach this small beach take Via di Posillipo until it becomes Discesa Coroglio, then take Via Marechiaro to the sea.
✉ Calata Ponticello 33 ☎ 081 769 1215

SCANDONE
Open-air, Olympic-sized pool near Edenlandia.
✉ Via dei Giochi del Mediterraneo, Fuorigrotta
☎ 081 570 2636 🕐 Open Jul and Aug only 🚋 Cavalleggeri D'Aosta 🚌 C9

STADIO SAN PAOLO
Napoli SSC soccer team plays here every other Sunday. Tickets from Azzurro Service (✉ Via F Galeota 17, Fuorigrotta ☎ 081 593 4001).
www.calcionapoli.it ✉ Piazzale Tecchio Fuorigrotta ☎ 081 239 5623 🚋 Mostra 🚋 Campi Flegrei 🚌 181, C9, C10

TENNIS CLUB NAPOLI
You don't have to belong to one of Naples' tennis clubs to get a game. You can also usually borrow rackets.
✉ Viale Anton Dohrn, Villa Comunale ☎ 081 761 4656
🚌 140, C9, C10, C24, C28, R3

VOLTURNO GOLF
The other golf course.
✉ Via Domitiana, Pinetamare Castelvolturno ☎ 081 509 5150/081 418 879

GYMS AND FITNESS CLUBS

Neapolitans are keen on fitness, provided it is stylish, so getting fit also involves seeing and being seen (especially when wearing the right brand). The main gyms in the city are:
Athena (✉ Via dei Mille 16 ☎ 081 407 334)
Bodyguard (✉ Via Torrione San Martino 45 ☎ 081 558 4551)
Centro Polisportivo Collana (✉ Via Rossini ☎ 081 560 1988)
Colosseum Gym (✉ Via Timavo 43)

Luxury Hotels

PRICES

Expect to pay over €120 per night for a luxury double room. (It is always worth asking when you make your reservation if any special deals are available.)

HOTELS IN POMPEI

Although it is easy to get to Pompei from Naples, an overnight stay can make the visit less of a rush. Most convenient is **Hotel Amleto** (**www**.hotelamleto.it ✉ Via B Longo 10 ☎ 081 863 1004), but slightly cheaper are **Hotel Forum** (**www**.hotelforum.it ✉ Via Roma 99 ☎ 081 850 1170), and **Villa Laura** (**www**.villalaura.com ✉ Via della Salle 13 ☎ 081 863 1024).

BRITANNIQUE

Set up high, this famous, elegant hotel has spectacular views, which can be enjoyed to the full from its own garden across the road.
info@hotelbritannique.it
✉ Corso V Emanuele 133
☎ 081 761 4145; fax 081 660 0457 🚇 C24, C27

CHIAIA HOTEL DE CHARME

In a very central Chiaia position, this splendid hotel is the converted home of Marquese Lecaldano (who lived here in the late 19th century). Many rooms have their original furniture, but the facilities are up to date.
www.hotelchiaia.it ✉ Via Chiaia 216 ☎ 081 415 555; fax 081 422 344 🚇 C22, C25, R3

EXCELSIOR

A very grand and elegant waterfront hotel. Rooms are blessed with period furnishings, fine paintings and huge luxurious beds. Many of them have a superb view across to Vesuvio.
www.excelsior.it ✉ Via Partenope 48 ☎ 081 764 0111; fax 081 764 9743 🚇 C25

GRAND HOTEL PARKER'S

A very luxurious hotel, Parker's enjoys marvellous views over the bay. There is an elegant 19th-century atmosphere, with chandeliers and antique furniture.
www.grandhotelparkers.it
✉ Corso Vittorio Emanuele 135
☎ 081 761 2474; fax 081 663 527 🚇 C24, C27

GRAND HOTEL VESUVIO

The oldest of the waterfront hotels, visited by royalty and politicians, this is traditionally furnished with every luxury and boasting a superb rooftop restaurant.
www.vesuvio.it ✉ Via Partenope 45 ☎ 081 764 0044; fax 081 764 4483 🚇 C25

MIRAMARE

A highly individual and most welcoming small hotel on the waterfront, which displays personal touches in each of the 30 rooms. Bedrooms are individually decorated, and there is an attractive roof terrace. Excellent service from the staff.
www.hotelmiramare.com ✉ Via N Sauro 24 ☎ 081 764 7589; fax 081 764 0775 🚇 C25

SAN FRANCESCO AL MONTE CONVENTO

This beautiful 16th-century monastery has been converted into a relaxing hotel with superb views from the terrace restaurant.
www.hotelsanfrancesco.it
✉ Corso Vittorio Emanuele 328
☎ 081 423 9111; fax 081 251 2485 🚇 C24, C27

SANTA LUCIA

A classical waterfront hotel with extremely elegant, spacious and comfortable rooms, filled with antique furniture. It occupies a splendid position overlooking Borgo Marinaro.
www.santalucia.it ✉ Via Partenope 46 ☎ 081 764 0666; fax 081 764 8580 🚇 C25

Mid-range Hotels

ALBERGO SANSEVERO

This atmospheric hotel across the road from the Piazza Bellini was converted from an 18th-century *palazzo*. The entrance is on the first floor (no lift/elevator), and the rooms are brightly decorated and well equipped.
www.albergosansevero.it ✉ Via Santa Maria Costantinopoli 101 ☎ 081 790 1000; fax 081 211 698 🚇 Dante 🚌 C57, E1, R1, R4

HOTEL DEL REAL ORTO BOTANICO

A restful hotel with an attractive terrace opposite the botanical gardens. It is tastefully furnished and is double glazed, which keeps out the traffic noise.
www.hotelrealortobotanico.it ✉ Via Foria 192 ☎ 081 442 1528; fax 081 442 1346 🚇 Piazza Cavour or Museo 🚌 14, 15, 47, 201, CS

HOTEL REX

Close to the sea on the Lungomare, this hotel has reasonably priced, brightly decorated rooms, some with balconies. The original ceiling paintings and the art nouveau decorations have been well restored after war damage.
www.hotel-rex.it ✉ Via Palepoli 12 ☎ 081 764 9389 🚌 C25

HOTEL SUITE ESEDRA

Very central, and close to Corso Umberto I, this hotel is a pleasant oasis away from the Neapolitan bustle. The rooms are generally small but they are smart and welcoming.
www.sea-hotels.com ✉ Via Cantani 12 ☎ 081 553 7087 🚇 Garibaldi 🚌 147, 148, R2

NAPOLIT'AMO

Housed in the handsome Palazzo Tocco di Montemiletto, this central hotel is good value. Rooms are high and bright, and there is internet access, and a garage.
www.napolitamo.it ✉ Via Toledo 148 ☎ 081 64 5462 🚇 Funicolare Augusteo 🚌 201, C25, C57, E3, E5, R3

NEAPOLIS

In the heart of the Centro Storico, this bright and welcoming hotel has modern facilities, and very helpful staff. The spacious rooms are all equipped with computers.
www.hotelneapolis.it ✉ Via Francesco del Giudice 13 ☎ 081 442 0815; fax 081 442 0819 🚇 Dante 🚌 E1, R4

PINTO STOREY

This charming old hotel on the fourth and fifth floors has been attractively refurbished while retaining its original character. Some rooms have a view over the city to the bay.
✉ Via Giuseppe Martucci 72 ☎ 081 681 260; fax 081 667 536 🚌 C24, C27

TOLEDO

This hotel has a very good location in a narrow street just off Via Toledo. Rooms are comfortable, and there is a charming roof garden.
✉ Via Montecalvario 15 ☎ 081 40 6800 🚇 Funicolare Augusteo 🚌 C25, C57, E3, E5, R3

PRICES

Expect to pay up to €120 per night for a double room in a mid-range hotel.

Budget Hotels

PRICES

Expect to pay up to €80 per night for a double room in a budget hotel.

BED AND BREAKFAST

Hotel accommodation in Naples is limited, and some of the cheaper hotels are not very classy, so it may be worth considering booking bed and breakfast. There are several agencies that do this. **Rent a Bed** (www.rentabed.com ✉ Vico Sergente Maggiore 16 ☎ 081 417 721) is efficient. Other good agencies are **My Home Your Home** (www.myhomeyourhome.it ✉ Via Duomo 276 ☎ 081 282 520), and **Associazone Bed & Breakfast** (www.tightrope.it/bbnaples/index.htm ✉ Cupa Camaldoli 18).

ALBERGO SANSEVERO DEGAS

Although the piazza outside the hotel can get noisy, the rooms are clean and pleasant, and you have the bonus of staying in a converted *palazzo* right in the heart of the Centro Storico.
www.albergosansevero.it
✉ Calata Trinità Maggiore 53
☎ 081 551 1276 Ⓜ Dante
🚌 E1, R4

AUSONIA

This is a clean and tidy *pensione* on the seafront in Mergellina. It is furnished with a nautical theme, but the rooms face onto the inner courtyard, so no great views. It is friendly and welcoming.
✉ Via Caracciolo 11 ☎ 081 66 45 36/081 68 22 78
Ⓜ Mergellina 🚌 C16, C24, R3

EUROPEO

There is inexpensive student-style accommodation in a good location at this very convenient but basic hotel. The rooms are modern and have air-conditioning, which is a bonus.
✉ Via Mezzocannone 109/C
☎ 081 551 7254 Ⓜ Dante
🚌 C36, E1

HOTEL DUOMO

Conveniently close to the cathedral and occupying the first floor in a quiet courtyard, this is a hospitable and inexpensive hotel. The rooms are clean, though basic, and the staff are helpful.
✉ Via Duomo 228 ☎ 081 265 988 🚌 148, C55, C58, R2

LA FONTANE DEL MARE

If you want sea views at a bargain price, you will find them here. Not all the rooms have their own bathrooms, and they are quite sparsely furnished, but the hotel is friendly. It is on the fifth floor, and you will need ten cents for the lift.
✉ Via Niccolo Tomasco 14
☎ 081 764 3811 🚌 C25, R3

MARGHERITA

A tiny hotel on the fifth floor of a *palazzo*. It has rather small rooms, but it is very welcoming and in a good position for shopping in Vomero, or taking the *Funicolare* down to via Toledo.
✉ Via Cimarosa 29 ☎ 081 556 7044 Ⓜ Funicolare Piazza Fuga 🚌 C25, C27

RUGGIERO

Bright, clean rooms are a feature of this welcoming hotel in the same building as the Pinto Storey. Some of them have good views over the city and most have bathrooms. It is close to Piazza Amedeo.
✉ Via Giuseppe Martucci 72
☎ 081 761 2460 🚌 C24, C27

SOGGIORNO SANSEVERO

The first floor of this 18th-century palazzo has been converted to an inexpensive *pensione*. Although the area is busy, the rooms face on to a quiet courtyard.
www.albergosansevero.it
✉ Piazza San Domenico Maggiore 9 ☎ 081 551 5949; fax 081 291 698 Ⓜ Dante
🚌 C36, E1

NAPLES
travel facts

ESSENTIAL FACTS

Customs regulations

- Duty-free limits for non-European Union visitors are 200 cigarettes or 50 cigars or 250g of tobacco; 2 litres of fortified wine and 1 litre of spirits (over 22 per cent alcohol).

Electricity

- Current is 220 volts AC (50 cycles), but is suitable for 240 volt devices.
- Plugs are of the Continental type with two round pins.
- British visitors should bring an adaptor.
- US visitors will need a voltage transformer.

Lavatories

- In bars and cafés ask for *il gabinetto* or *il bagno*.
- Do not confuse *signori* (men) with *signore* (women).

Money matters

- Credit cards: Major cards are widely accepted and can be used in ATMs displaying the appropriate sign
- Travellers' cheques: Most major travellers' cheques can be changed at banks
- Foreign exchange: Facilities are available at banks and kiosks

Opening hours

- Banks: Mon–Fri 8.30–1.15, 2.15–3.30.
- Churches: Published opening times may vary according to who is on duty. Many churches close at 1 or 1.30.
- Museums and attractions: Major attractions stay open all day, but generally close one day per week (see individual details).
- Post Offices: Mon–Fri 8.15–7, Sat 8.15–12.
- Restaurants: 12.30–3.30, 7.30–10.30 or later. Some restaurants do not open for lunch. Many close for all or part of Aug.
- Shops: Mon–Sat 8.30–1.30, 4.30–7. Non-food shops often close Mon morning. Some food shops open Sun morning and close Thu or Sat afternoon. Many shops close in Aug.

Places of worship

- Anglican: Christ Church
  ✉ Via San Pasquale a Chiaia 15
  ☎ 081 411 842
- Baptist: ✉ Via Foria 93
  ☎ 081 287 650
- Jewish: ✉ Via Santa Maria a Cappella Vecchia 31 ☎ 081 764 3480

Public holidays

- 1 Jan: New Year's Day
- 6 Jan: Epiphany (*Befana*)
- Easter Sunday
- Easter Monday
- 25 Apr: Liberation Day
- 1 May: Labour Day
- 15 Aug: Assumption (*Ferragosto*)
- 1 Nov: All Saints' Day
- 8 Dec: Immaculate Conception
- 25 Dec: Christmas Day
- 26 Dec: Santo Stefano

(Good Friday is not a holiday).

Safety

- In spite of its reputation, Naples is no more dangerous than other large cities. It is sensible to keep money and valuables well hidden, and not to carry bags so that they can be easily stolen. Shoulder bags should be slung across the body; backpacks are as vulnerable here as anywhere.
- Keep on the inside of pavements.
- Never keep valuables in your car; always lock the car doors.

Smoking

- Not permitted in bars, restaurants, public transport or taxis, but plenty of people do it.

Student visitors

- Campsites: Averno ✉ Via Montenuovo Licola Patria 85, Arco Felice, Pozzuoli ☎ 081 804 2666; Vulcano Solfatara ✉ Via Solfatara, Pozzuoli ☎ 081 526 7413
- Youth hostel: ✉ Salita della Grotta a Piedigrotta 23 ☎ 081 761 2346

Tipping

- Bars, restaurants: 15–20 per cent
- Taxis: 15–20 per cent
- Chambermaids: €5
- Hairdressers: €3
- Porters: €2
- Cloakroom attendants: €1

Women visitors

- Neapolitan men will sometimes try to speak to unaccompanied women, but generally can be rebuffed easily. The main area to avoid is around Piazza Garibaldi and the Stazione Centrale, which is seedy by day and unpleasant by night.

MEDIA & COMMUNICATIONS

Newspapers and magazines

- All Italian daily papers are available, and so are most major European and American titles (which can usually be bought after about 2.30 on the day of issue from booths (*edicole*) in the city). Most popular is *Il Mattino*, which has good listings of cinemas, playhouses and music.
- Good free papers available in the city in the mornings are *City* and *Leggo*, which have useful music sections. Indispensable is the free monthly tourist magazine *Qui Napoli*.

Post offices

- Central Post Office: ✉ Piazza Matteoti ☎ 081 551 1456 🕐 Mon–Fri 8.15–7, Sat 8.15–12.
- Mail boxes: Red, usually with two slots—*città* and *altre destinazioni*.
- First-class mail: Generally good—24 hours in Italy, three days to EU countries, longer elsewhere.
- More information: www.poste.it; helpline ☎ 160.

Radio

- RAI, the state broadcaster, runs three radio stations.
- American Forces Network has two stations.
- Independent stations are numerous, and the most popular is *Kiss Kiss Napoli*.

Telephones

- Outgoing: To call UK ☎ 0044, to call US ☎ 001, to call Australia ☎ 0061, to call Irish Republic ☎ 00353
- Incoming: To call Italy from home the country code is 39. All numbers in Naples start with ☎ 081.
- Toll-free numbers: Start with ☎ 800.
- International operator: ☎ 170.
- International directory enquiries: ☎ 176.

Television

- RAI, the state broadcaster, has three channels.
- Mediasetonline runs three channels.

EMERGENCIES

Emergency phone numbers

- Police ☎ 112
- Ambulance ☎ 118
- Fire ☎ 115
- Car breakdown ☎ 116
- Coastguard ☎ 1530
- General emergencies ☎ 113

Consulates

- Canada: ✉ Via Carducci 29 ☎ 081 401 338
- France: ✉ Via Crispi 86 ☎ 081 598 0711
- Germany: ✉ Via Crispi 69 ☎ 081 248 8511
- Japan: ✉ Via Ponte di Tappia 82 ☎ 081 552 1183
- Spain: ✉ Via dei Mille 40 ☎ 081 411 157
- United Kingdom: ✉ Via dei Mille 40 ☎ 081 423 8911
- United States: ✉ Piazza della Repubblica ☎ 081 583 8111

Lost property

- Lost property can sometimes be traced through the relevant lost property offices at the airport, or Stazione Centrale, or at the terminus of the bus line you were using.
- Stolen property should be reported to the police on ☎ 112, or to the nearest police station, and a record obtained for insurance purposes.

Medical and dental treatment

- Emergency dentist: ☎ 081 664 436 or in emergency go to Ospedale Cardarelli.
- Emergency doctor: ☎ 081 761 3466.
- Hospitals: Ospedale Cardarelli ✉ Via Antonio Cardarelli 9 ☎ 081 546 4318; Ospedale Santobono ✉ Via Mario Fiore ☎ 081 220 5111.
- Medicines: Pharmacists will make up your prescriptions and give general medical advice. They may also sell homeopathic medicines.
- Pharmacists: Identified by their large green cross ⊙ Mon–Fri 8.30–1, 4–8, Sat 8.30–1.

VISITOR INFORMATION

- Bus information: www.anm.it or ☎ 800 639 525

- Funicolare information: ☎ 800 568 866
- Magazine: *Qui Napoli* monthly magazine available from tourist offices, or downloaded from www.inaples.it
- Metro information: ☎ 800 568 886
- Telephone information: ☎ 800 251 396
- Tourist information can be obtained from the following places: ✉ Piazza del Gesù Nuovo ☎ 081 552 3328 ⊙ Mon–Sat 9–8, Sun 9–3; ✉ Portico di San Francesco di Paola, Piazza del Plebiscito ☎ 081 247 1123 ⊙ Mon–Fri 9–7, Sat 9–2; ✉ Piazza dei Martiri 58 ☎ 081 405 311 ⊙ Mon–Fri 8–3.30. There are other tourist information points at Stazione Centrale, Mergellina station and Capodichino airport.
- Traffic information: ☎ 166 664 477
- Train (Circumvesuviana) information: ☎ 081 772 2444
- Train (Cumana) information: www.sepsa.it ☎ 800 551 3328
- Water taxi information: ☎ 081 877 3600.

LANGUAGE

- Once you have mastered a few basic rules, Italian is an easy language to speak: It is phonetic, and unlike English, particular combinations of letters are always pronounced the same way. The stress is usually on the penultimate syllable, but if the word has an accent, this is where the stress falls.
- All Italian nouns are either masculine (usually ending in o when singular or i when plural) or feminine (usually ending in a when singular or e when plural). Some nouns, which may be masculine or feminine, end in e (which changes to i when plural). An adjective's ending changes to match the ending of the noun.

Useful Phrases

what is the time? che ore sono?
when do you open/close? a che ora apre/chiude?
I don't speak Italian non parlo italiano
do you speak English? parla inglese?
I don't understand non capisco
what does this mean? cosa significa questo?
my name is mi chiamo
what's your name? come si chiama?
hello, pleased to meet you piacere
I live in ... vivo in ...
I'm here on holiday sono qui in vacanza
good morning buongiorno
good afternoon/evening buona sera
goodbye arrivederci
see you later a più tardi
see you tomorrow a domani
see you soon a presto
how are you? come sta?
fine, thank you bene, grazie
I'm sorry mi dispiace

Useful Words

yes sì
no no
please per piacere
thank you grazie
you're welcome prego
excuse me! scusi!
where dove
here qui
there là
when quando
now adesso
later più tardi
why perchè
who chi
may I/can I posso

Numbers

one uno
two due
three tre
four quattro
five cinque
six sei
seven sette
eight otto
nine nove
ten dieci
eleven undici
twelve dodici
thirteen tredici
fourteen quattordici
fifteen quindici
sixteen sedici
seventeen diciassette
eighteen diciotto
nineteen diciannove
twenty venti

Days of the Week

Monday lunedì
Tuesday martedì
Wednesday mercoledì
Thursday giovedì
Friday venerdì
Saturday sabato
Sunday domenica

Emergencies

help! aiuto!
stop, thief! al ladro!
can you help me, please? può aiutarmi, per favore?
call the fire brigade/police/an ambulance chiami i pompieri/la polizia/un'ambulanza
I have lost my passport/ wallet/purse/handbag ho perso il passaporto/il portafoglio/il borsellino/la borsa
where is the police station? dov'è il commissariato?
I have been robbed sono stato/a derubato/a
I have had an accident ho avuto un incidente
where is the hospital? dov'è l'ospedale?
I don't feel well non mi sento bene
could you call a doctor please può chiamare un medico, per favore
first aid pronto soccorso

93

Index

Citypack
naples' 25 best

Author Michael Buttler
Contributions by Anna Maria d'Angelo
Cover Design Tigist Getachew, Fabrizio La Rocca

ISBN 1-4000-1517-0

FIRST EDITION

ACKNOWLEDGMENTS
The Automobile Association would like to thank the following libraries, agencies and photographers for their assistance in the preparation of this book.
Corbis 29t, 29b, 31, 39, 54, 55; John Heseltine Archive 28, 45; Hutchinson Picture Library 35; Marka 38, 40, 47, 53, 56; Scala Archives 49t, 49b; Stockbyte 5; The Travel Library 32, 33; World Pictures 24, 26.

The remaining pictures are held in the Association's own library (AA WORLD TRAVEL LIBRARY) and were taken by Max Jourdan, with the exception of 51t, which was taken by Clive Sawyer, and 8cb and 34, which were taken by Tony Souter.

IMPORTANT TIP
Time inevitably brings changes, so always confirm prices, travel facts, and other perishable information when it matters. Although Fodor's cannot accept responsibility for errors, you can use this guide in the confidence that we have taken every care to ensure its accuracy.

SPECIAL SALES
This book is available for special discounts for bulk purchases for sales promotions or premiums. Special editions, including personalized covers, excerpts of existing books, and corporate imprints, can be created in large quantities for special needs. For more information, write to Special Markets/ Premium Sales, 1745 Broadway, MD 6-2, New York, NY 10019 or e-mail: specialmarkets@randomhouse.com.

Colour separation by Keenes, Andover, United Kingdom.
Printed in Hong Kong by Hang Tai D&P Limited
10 9 8 7 6 5 4 3 2 1

AO1998
Maps in this title produced from mapping © Mairs Geographischer Verlag / Falk Verlag, 73751 Ostfildern, Germany
Fold out map © Mairs Geographischer Verlag / Falk Verlag, 73751 Ostfildern, Germany

TITLES IN THE CITYPACK SERIES
• Amsterdam • Bangkok • Barcelona • Beijing • Berlin • Boston • Brussels & Bruges • Chicago • Dublin •
• Florence • Hong Kong • Lisbon • London • Los Angeles • Madrid • Melbourne • Miami • Milan •
• Montréal • Munich • Naples • New York • Paris • Prague • Rome • San Francisco • Seattle • Shanghai •
• Singapore • Sydney • Tokyo • Toronto • Venice • Vienna • Washington DC •